In memoriam

NORMAN A. ROBERTSON
1892–1962

The Song of Roland
La Chanson de Roland

Translated with an Introduction and Notes by
HOWARD S. ROBERTSON
Professor of French, Glendon College, York University,
Toronto

J. M. Dent & Sons Ltd, London

NO. 777   ISBN: 0 460 00777 7
NO. 1777   ISBN: 0 460 01777 2

CONTENTS

v

I should like to acknowledge the encouragement of Professor D. G. Mowatt of the University of Newcastle, Australia, the patience and suggestions of my wife who read the entire manuscript, and the efforts of Mrs Monique Gyalokay and Miss Elizabeth Gyalokay who typed and proofread the drafts.

H. S. R.

INTRODUCTION

At the close of the eleventh century an unknown poet, perhaps named Turoldus, composed the work we call the *Chanson de Roland*. Although the legend of Roland was well known in mediaeval times, and its hero frequently cited as a model of chivalry, it was the publication in 1837 by Francisque Michel of the earliest, most complete and most literate manuscript that gained the attention of modern readers. Digby 23, as the manuscript is called, is about the size of a modern pocketbook and almost devoid of ornamentation. It was written in England between 1130 and 1150 and belongs to the Bodleian Library at Oxford. Despite the existence of six other manuscripts and some fragments, this manuscript forms the basis of the editions in which the poem has principally been read and studied.

We have no knowledge of the direct sources of the poem and little of the history of the legend. Eginhard's *Vita Caroli* (ca 830) states that on 15th August 778 the entire Frankish rearguard, among them Rolandus, Count of the March of Brittany, was wiped out by Basques while covering the return of Charlemagne's army over the Pyrenees from its expedition in Spain. Legend apparently enlarged and ornamented subsequent accounts of the event and other versions doubtless circulated. The mediaeval historian Wace says that Taillefer, William the Conqueror's minstrel, sang a song of Roland to the troops at Hastings. Other partial versions, later than our poem, are the Latin *Carmen de Proditione Guenonis* of the mid-twelfth century and the *Historia Caroli Magni et Rothlandi* (often called the *Pseudo-Turpin*), a prose work of the same period. Roland's deeds have been immortalized in the stained glass windows of the basilica of Saint Denis and the cathedral of Chartres.

The poem here translated opens with a political problem: should Charlemagne, after seven years of war, complete his conquest of the Saracen-held old Christian kingdoms of Spain by laying siege to the Saracen leader, King Marsilie,

in Saragossa, his heavily fortified capital? The council of
Frankish barons, led by Duke Naimes and Count Ganelon,
advises a treaty, peace and a return to France; Count
Roland, Ganelon's stepson and Charlemagne's nephew,
advocates the reduction of Saragossa and total military
victory. The peace party prevails, but Ganelon, at Roland's
suggestion, is named ambassador to Marsilie—a dangerous
mission, since the Saracen king murdered the previous
Frankish ambassadors in the course of earlier negotiations.

The personal quarrel between stepfather and stepson
leads Ganelon to challenge Roland and his followers in an
open feud and then to betray the young hero to Marsilie.
Roland will, on Ganelon's recommendation, command the
rearguard as the Franks return home; Marsilie agrees to
slaughter Roland and his men, thus hopefully depriving
Charlemagne of his top field commander, his favourite knights
(the Twelve Peers) and Roland's twenty thousand French
knights.

All turns out as planned. Because of Roland's proud
refusal to call for reinforcements and despite magnificent
personal bravery on the part of the French, the rearguard
is overwhelmed and slaughtered to a man. Roland, however,
had consented to sound his horn late in the battle and the
Saracens, after one last attempt to kill Roland, flee the
battlefield. Roland lives long enough to watch them go;
he claims the victory, confesses his sins, and angels descend
from heaven to claim his soul. On hearing the horn, Charlemagne suspects the worst and arrests Ganelon; the army
returns to Rencesvals, defeats Marsilie with God's help and
avenges Roland.

Suddenly, Marsilie's long-awaited reinforcements arrive:
his liege lord Baligant, Emir of Cairo, with a vast army.
Deprived of his field commander and despite apparent great
age, Charlemagne assumes vigorous command himself.
Aided by God again, he defeats Baligant's army in a long
and bloody battle, killing the Emir with his own hand.
Saragossa is taken, its population converted or killed, and
its queen led off to France by Charlemagne.

Once back at Aix, Charlemagne opens Ganelon's trial,

accusing him of treason through his destruction of Roland and his followers. Ganelon defends himself courageously and the council, deciding in his favour, attempts a reconciliation. But an unlikely champion, Tierri, appears for the emperor's case and demands trial by combat. In the ensuing duel, Ganelon's champion, the magnificent Pianbel, is killed contrary to all expectations and Charlemagne's cause is upheld. Ganelon and thirty of his supporters are promptly executed.

Just as a peaceful life seems imminent, God sends Charlemagne news of a Christian king requiring aid. The emperor laments his difficult life and prepares once again to obey. Here ends the tale.

The *Roland* has been the focus of much controversy, all scholarly, mainly historical. Hailed by the French as their great national epic, it was studied less as a poem than as a document of eleventh- and twelfth-century life and thought. Efforts to search out its genesis and to reconstruct the poem's 'original' form on the basis of all the manuscripts tended to obscure its literary value. The great exception to this situation was the work of Joseph Bédier (1864–1938). While his *Les Légendes épiques* (first edition 1908–13) dealt with the origins of the epic and of the *Roland* in particular, he viewed the version of Digby 23 as the work of a single literary artist and never lost sight of the poem's literary importance; many of his analyses remain unsurpassed. Bédier's partisans have become known as 'individualists'; those who prefer to see the *Roland* as a compilation of tales from traditional songs and legends (no trace of which exists), and the poet as a more or less awkward compiler, have been dubbed 'traditionalists'. These two views have largely polarized thought for the last fifty years. Recent criticism, particularly the New Criticism in England and North America, has followed the spirit of Bédier's half-century-old enunciation of the importance of viewing the poem as a whole; neo-traditionalists (for example, the late Ramon Menendez-Pidal) rise from time to time offering challenge. The struggle appears endless.

Interpretations have seen the title as a misnomer, preferring to view the poem as a 'Chanson de Charlemagne', with Roland as an essentially episodic figure; another sees a religious parallel: Roland as Christ figure, Charlemagne as God figure, Ganelon as Judas, etc.; an older view is that the poem is really a celebration of the epic hero and a bit of crusade propaganda to stir up twelfth-century Frenchmen to take arms against Islam. The critical literature is vast and impossible to summarize here. The present translator sees the poem as a complex story where little is black and white and which presents less a celebration of the hero than an examination of his role. We are offered a portrait of the great emperor, defender of France and of Christianity, surrounded by quarrelling barons, beleaguered by his enemies, torn between his own loves and loyalties and the duties of his office. The poem begins and ends with the tragic and human monarch called upon to perform the super-human, even at God's direct bidding. Roland the hero, bearing the burden of being a legend in his own time, clearly presents the problem of whether one can be a hero and perform the near impossible while remaining true to other ideals of humility, concern for one's fellow and the general good. His companion Oliver is more concerned with commonsense survival, the importance of living and strategic responsibility; but for all his bravery and perhaps because of these concerns, he does not reach the heights of Roland's victory, death and reward. A major concern of the poem is the complication of a man of unquestioned stature, nobility and reputation who stoops to personal jealousy and revenge when confronted by the hero who puts his own legend before all else. Ganelon's betrayal of Roland raises the fine point of whether he is really guilty of treason against his liege lord Charlemagne. The personal tone of the emperor's prosecution of Ganelon at the end of the poem leaves much for the reader to ponder concerning the ambiguities of justice. Finally, the poem is set in a framework of brave men who do their duty and die for the causes they can believe in.

Despite the occasional tedium of the naming of the knights and the lengthy battle scenes somewhat routinely described, there runs through the poem a counterpoint of excitement

and tragedy: the thrill of the campaign, personal confronta-
tions, the battles and their outcome, the tragedy of the
monarch, the death of noble and brave men, and the passing
of the hero. The psychology of treason, the extremities of
Saracen desperation, the subtleties of diplomacy, the
politics of the council meeting, the generation gap between
young and old, between reckless and established, all provide
the reader with an endless source of meditation on the
stresses of the human condition in epic circumstances.

HOWARD S. ROBERTSON

Glendon College, York University, Toronto
1972

SELECT BIBLIOGRAPHY

No selection can do justice to the vast literature of the
Roland, but the following works may prove of interest to the
student and the general reader.

EDITIONS

F. Whitehead, *La Chanson de Roland*, Blackwell's French
Texts, Oxford, 2nd ed., 1946.

Joseph Bédier, *La Chanson de Roland*, Piazza, Paris, 1922,
and *La Chanson de Roland Commentée* (referred to in this
translation's Notes as '*Commentaire*'), Piazza, Paris, 1927.

T. Atkinson Jenkins, *La Chanson de Roland*, rev. ed.,
New York, 1929.

ORIGINS OF THE EPIC AND COMMENTARY

Joseph Bédier, *Les légendes epiques*, 4 vols., 3rd ed., Paris, 1926–9.

Urban T. Holmes, Jr., 'The Post-Bédier theories on the origins of the *chansons de geste*', *Speculum*, XXX (1955), 72–81.

Ramon Menendez-Pidal, *La Chanson de Roland et la tradition épique des Francs*, trans. by I. M. Cluzel, Paris, 1960.

RECENT INTERPRETATIONS AND COMMENTARY

D. D. R. Owen, 'The Secular inspiration of the *Chanson de Roland*', *Speculum*, XXXVII (1962), 390–400.

Alain Renoir, 'Roland's lament: its meaning and function in the *Chanson de Roland*', *Speculum* XXXV (1960), 573–83.

Robert A. Hall, 'Linguistic Strata in the *Chanson de Roland*', *Romance Philology* XIII (1959), 156–61.

Janet W. Boatner, 'The Misunderstood Ordeal: a Re-examination of the *Chanson de Roland*', *Studies in Philology* LXVI (1969), 571–83.

André de Mandach, *Naissance et développement de la chanson de geste en Europe*. I. *La geste de Charlemagne et de Roland*, Paris & Geneva, 1961.

Howard S. Robertson, 'Blancandrin as Diplomat', *Romance Notes* X, 2 (1969), 372–78.

Eugene Vance, *Reading the Song of Roland*, New Jersey, 1970.

TRANSLATIONS INTO ENGLISH

Verse, Charles Scott-Moncrieff, 1919; Dorothy L. Sayers, 1957.

Prose, René Hague (with Oxford text), 1937.

NOTE TO THE TRANSLATION

All literary translations are interpretations. Only the diffuse
and detailed exploration of the classroom or the public lec-
ture can aspire to account for all the possibilities inherent
in a poem. The attempts of many translations to reproduce
in some manner the 'flavour' or the 'effect' of the original
poem always wind up presenting but one view and one
interpretation. The effect of the original, however, must
always have been multiple. Mediaeval listeners of varying
sophistication and modern scholars since, equipped with a
knowledge of the language, must have had different re-
actions, their perspectives being different.

Reproductions of the 'original flavour' of the poem
frequently take the form of archaisms and a syntax which
belongs to no readily identifiable period of the English
language. Efforts to assonance the English in imitation of
the Old French usually offer only the insipidity of impure
rhyme where the original possesses richness and variety.
The present translation attempts first and foremost to
convey the notion that the original is a poem, and a poem
of great power but simple diction. Blank verse seems best
able to present the decasyllabic original—the metre being
loosened by irregularities to allow for changes of stress and
to avoid monotony. The English diction is mainly a contemporary form of the language in preference to an heroic
archaism better described as 'dateless' than 'timeless'. The
archaisms, usually syntactical, are due to the metre and are
unsought. Wherever possible, the straight English equiva-
lent is used in preference to some *recherché* interpretation:
Roland 'sounds' or 'blows' his horn; there is no need to
have him 'wind' it.

Since some readers may wish to use the translation along
with the original, the lines are in their proper order, the
content of one rarely spilling over into the next. The English
version is based, with the permission of Basil Blackwell &
Mott Ltd, Oxford, on the readily available edition by Professor F. Whitehead, published by Blackwell's French Texts,

xiii

to which our notes make frequent reference. The translation is as literal as common sense and the metre will allow, the great exception being the variation in Old French verb tenses. While literalness would be served if the English verb tenses corresponded exactly with the Old French, the tenses of Old French are frequently in strange sequence and the corresponding English would appear bizarre.

The subtlety of the poem must have afforded ample scope to any jongleur who sang or recited it in mediaeval times. An ironical accent here, a shift of facial expression there, and the individual episodes, hence whole sections of the poem, could assume a different cast. Readers and translators ever since, according to the circumstances which formed them, have never ceased to reinterpret the *Chanson de Roland*. While this translation must interpret, within its broad limits the reader may form his own interpretation. Indeed, that is his responsibility.

The Song of Roland

La Chanson de Roland

In this translation, *Marsilie* is disyllabic as it is in Old French, the final *i* being a yod (consonantal *i*) and the final *e* virtually mute. Similarly, *Suatilie* v. 90, *Sezilie* v. 200, *Basilie* v. 207, *Haltilie* v. 208. *Ganelon* is usually disyllabic, sometimes trisyllabic. The use of diaeresis marks all other departures from appearances, e.g., *Anseïs* v. 105, *Préciuse* v. 3146.

THE SONG OF ROLAND

I

King Charlemagne, our noble emperor,
Has been in Spain for fully seven years
And conquered the high country to the sea.
No castle stands before his army now;
5 No wall or city left for him to crush
Except, atop a mountain, Saragoce,
The seat of King Marsilie who loves not God;
He serves Mahomet, to Apollo prays;
*He cannot help disaster reaching him. Aoi.

II

10 The king Marsilie held court at Saragoce.
Within a garden, underneath the shade,
†He sits upon a throne of yellow marble,
Around him more than twenty thousand men.
He speaks thus to his dukes and to his counts:
15 'Hear me, my lords, what trouble now surrounds us.
Great Charles, the emperor, from his sweet France
Comes to confound us and destroy our land.
I have no army that can give him battle,
I have no forces fit to break his own.
20 Advise me now as you are my wise men
And so protect me from both death and shame.'
No pagan answers him a single word
Save Blancandrin of Castel de Valfunde.

III

The wisest of the pagans, Blancandrin
25 —Most knightly in performance of his tasks,
A man of valour fit to serve his lord—
Spoke to the king: 'Now do not be afraid.
Send word to Charles, that proud and haughty king,
Assuring him great friendship, faithful service.
30 Say that you'll send him bears and lions and dogs,
Seven hundred camels and a thousand falcons,

Four hundred mules laden with gold and silver,
Full fifty cartloads he may bear away;
From that he'll have enough to pay his soldiers!
35   Remind him of the length of his campaign,
Suggest that he return to France, to Aix;
And you will follow at Saint Michael's feast
There to receive the Christian law and faith
And be his vassal, loyal and sincere.
40   If he wants hostages, you'll send him some—
Or ten, or twenty—as a pledge of faith.
*We'll send to him our firstborn sons, our heirs;
Though he should die for it, I'll send my own.
Better by far that they should lose their heads
45   Than all of us our power and prestige,
Or that we should be brought to beggary.' AOI.

IV

Said Blancandrin, 'I swear by my right hand
And by the beard that waves upon my chest
You'll see their host decamping straightaway.
50   *Franks will return to France, to their own land.
When each will be at home, at his own seat—
And Charlemagne at his, Aix-la-Chapelle—
He'll hold the great feast on Saint Michael's day.
The day will come and the appointed hour
55   Without his having word or news of us.
The king is proud and terrible his heart;
He'll cut the heads off all our hostages.
Better by far that they should lose their heads
Than we should lose our beautiful bright Spain
60   Or bear privation, evil, want and grief.'
The pagans answer, 'It may well be so!'

V

The king Marsilie first heard his council out.
Then he called forth Clarin de Balaguer,
Estamarin and Eudropin his peer,
65   With Priamum he called bearded Guarlun,
And Machiner and his uncle Maheu,
Jouner, Malbien from far beyond the seas,

And Blancandrin to bear his words to Charles.
†Of the most wicked, he chose these ten lords.
70 'My lords,' he says, 'you'll go to Charlemagne,
Who even now is laying siege to Cordres,
Bearing these olive branches in your hands
To signify humility and peace.
If by your wisdom you can bring accord,
75 I'll freely grant you gifts: silver and gold,
Both lands and fiefs as much as you could wish.'
*The pagans answer, 'These we have in plenty.' Aoi.

VI

The king Marsilie had heard his council speak
Then said to his men: 'My lords, you now will go
80 With olive branches waving in your hands
And say to Charlemagne on my behalf
For his God's love that he should show me mercy.
Before this coming month has passed away,
I, with a thousand of my faithful men,
85 Will follow him and take the Christian faith.
Love and my oath shall bind me to his service.
If he wants hostages, he'll have enough.'
Said Blancandrin, 'We shall plead well for you.' Aoi.

VII

The king Marsilie had ten white mules led out
90 —Sent to him by the King of Suatilie,
Their reins of gold, their saddles silver wrought—
To serve as mounts for his ambassadors
Who, bearing olive branches in their hands,
Journeyed to Charles who holds France in his sway;
95 He cannot help but that they will deceive him. Aoi.

VIII

The emperor's mood is jubilant and joyous;
Cordres is taken and its walls are pierced,
His catapults have broken down its towers,
His knights have taken out enormous booty
100 Of gold and silver, richest ornaments.

Within the town no pagan now remains:
Death or baptism was all the choice they had.
The emperor is resting in a garden;
With him are Roland and Count Oliver,
105 Sansun the duke and the proud Anseïs,
Godefroy d'Anjou who bears the gonfanon,
Gerin, Gerer are of their company
With many others grouped around, in all,
Some fifteen thousand nobles of sweet France.
110 The knights are sitting on white silken cloths.
While some amuse themselves at gambling—
The wiser, older men are playing chess—
It's fencing for the lively younger knights.
Under a pine, beside a wild brier bush,
115 Upon a faldstool wrought in purest gold
Sits Charlemagne, the king who rules all France.
White is his beard and hoary is his head,
His stature noble and his countenance proud—
No need to point him out to any man.
120 The envoys from Marsilie dismount and greet him
With protestations of good will and love.

IX

The pagan Blancandrin, the first to speak,
Says to the king: 'Blessings on you from God,
The glorious one whom we should all adore.
125 Here are the words of noble King Marsilie:
Much has he sought concerning your religion;
Of his own wealth he wants to make you presents:
Bears, lions and chained hounds he offers you,
Seven hundred camels and a thousand falcons,
130 Four hundred mules with gold and silver laden,
And fifty carts for you to bear away.
Among the treasure, besants of pure gold
Enough to pay your soldiers every one.
You have been in our country overlong;
135 To France, to Aix, you might now well return.
My lord will follow you, upon his oath.'
The emperor holds up his hands to God;
Lowering his head, to ponder he begins. Aoi.

X

The emperor remained with his head bowed
140 And in no hurry to reveal his mind.
His wont is to express himself at leisure.
When he looks up, his face is proud and grim.
He says to the envoys, 'You have spoken well.
But King Marsilie is still my enemy;
145 And all these fine words you have spoken here,
To what extent may I believe in them?'
'Through hostages,' replied the Saracen,
'Some ten, fifteen, or twenty you will have.
I'll place my son among those risking death;
150 You could not have, I think, a nobler lot.
When to your royal palace you've returned,
The day you celebrate Saint Michael's feast,
My suzerain takes oath to follow you
And, in the baths made for you there by God,
155 Willingly to become a Christian man.'
Charles answers, 'Even yet he may be saved.' Aoi.

XI

The evening light was clear and beautiful.
Charles has the ten mules stabled for the night
And in a garden orders a tent pitched
160 Where he may lodge the ten ambassadors.
Twelve of his soldiers see to all their needs;
They stay the night until the morning breaks.
The emperor has risen very early;
He has attended mass and matins both
165 And then resumed his seat beneath the pine,
Calling his lords to give their final word:
On their advice alone will he proceed. Aoi.

XII

The emperor takes his seat beneath a pine,
Calls on his lords for definite advice:
170 Archbishop Turpin and the duke Oger,
Richard the Old and his nephew Henry,
Noble Acelin, the count of Gascony,
Tedbald de Reins, his cousin lord Milun;

Both Gerer and Gerin were present there,
175 Roland the count appeared along with them
And Oliver, the valiant, noble man.
More than a thousand Franks of France assembled;
Among them was the traitor Ganelon.
And now begins the council that went wrong. Aoi.

XIII

180 'My lords and barons,' says the emperor Charles,
'The king Marsilie has sent ambassadors.
He wants to give me much of his own wealth:
Lions and bears, a number of trained hounds,
Seven hundred camels and a thousand falcons,
185 Four hundred mules laden with Arab gold,
And in addition more than fifty carts.
But he suggests that I return to France;
There he will follow me to my abode;
He will receive, he says, our healing faith,
190 Become a Christian, hold his lands from me.
And yet, I wonder what is in his heart.'
The French reply, 'We must be on our guard.' Aoi.

XIV

The emperor has finished his review.
Count Roland, who does not agree at all,
195 Gets to his feet and speaks against this course.
He says to Charles: 'You must not trust Marsilie.
We came to Spain full seven years ago.
I conquered for you Noples and Commibles,
Then took Valterne and all the land of Pine,
200 And Balaguer, with Tüele and Sezilie.
Marsilie's response was purest treachery.
He sent us fifteen of his pagan host
—Each bore a branch of olive in his hand—
Who then addressed you with these selfsame words.
205 You sought advice, consulting with your Franks
Who counselled you to take a foolish course:
You sent two counts as envoys to Marsilie
—One was Basan, the other one Basilie—

He took their heads on the hills above Haltilie!
210 Now fight the war as you have undertaken!
Lead on your gathered host to Saragoce!
Lay siege to it though it take all your life!
Avenge those whom the felon put to death!' Aoɪ.

XV

The emperor remains with his head bowed,
215 Smoothing his moustache, stroking his white beard,
Answering his nephew neither 'yes' nor 'no'.
The French are silent, save for Ganelon.
He rises to his feet, comes before Charles,
And proudly, forcefully begins his speech,
220 Saying to the king, 'You must not trust a fool,
Myself or others, except to your advantage.
Now when the king Marsilie sends word to you
That he will swear, hands joined, to be your vassal
And hold all Spain a fief, a gift from you,
225 And then receive the faith to which we cling—
He, who advises we reject this plea,
He does not care by what death we may die!
A counsel based on pride should not prevail.
Let us forget the fools; hold to the wise!' Aoɪ.

XVI

230 After this speech duke Naimes presents himself
—No better vassal ever was in court—
And says to the king, 'You've listened carefully
To what Count Ganelon has said to you.
There's wisdom in it, only give it heed!
235 The king Marsilie is beaten in this war:
All of his castles have you taken from him;
Your catapults have broken down his walls;
You've burned his cities and you've killed his men.
Now since he asks that you should show him mercy,
240 Who would fight on invites calamity . . .
With hostages he gives you guarantees.
This great war should not be continued further.'
*The French agree, 'The duke has spoken well.' Aoɪ.

XVII

'My lords and barons, whom then shall we send
245 To Saragoce to see the king Marsilie?'
Duke Naimes responds, 'I shall go, by your leave.
*Give me now for this mission glove and staff.'
'You are too wise a man,' replies the king,
'I swear by both my moustache and my beard,
250 You'll never go that far away from me.
Go take your seat, since no one summons you.'

XVIII

'My lords and barons, say whom can we send
To the Saracen who rules in Saragoce?'
Roland responds, 'I'm quite prepared to go.'
255 'Indeed no!' interrupts Count Oliver,
'Your disposition is too fierce and proud.
I fear you'd only get embroiled and fight.
If the king pleases, I can go myself.'
But the king answers, 'Both of you be still!
260 Neither of you will set a foot up there!
By this beard you see whitening day by day,
My own twelve peers will not be given this task!'
The French fall silent, crushed beneath his words.

XIX

Turpin de Reins has risen from his seat
265 And says to the king, 'Do not berate your Franks.
Seven long years you have been in this land;
Much pain and hardship have they suffered here,
Give me, my lord, the glove and the baton;
I shall go to this Saracen of Spain
270 †And try to read his purpose in his face.'
The emperor replies with sudden anger,
'Go and sit down upon your silken cloth
And speak no more unless I bid you to.' Aoi.

XX

'My noble knights,' repeats the emperor Charles,
275 'Select for me a lord of my domain

To carry my reply to King Marsilie.'
Says Roland, 'My stepfather, Ganelon!'
The French advise, 'Indeed a fitting choice!
Let him but go, you'll send no wiser man.'
280 But Ganelon leaps up in great distress,
Hurling aside his robe of marten furs,
And stands respendent in his silken tunic,
His eyes ablaze, his face both proud and fierce.
Noble is he of body, strongly built,
285 So handsome that his peers can only gaze.
He calls to Roland, 'Fool! Why do you rage?
Everyone knows that I am your stepfather,
Yet you propose that I go to Marsilie.
If God but grant that I return from there,
290 I'll undertake against you such a feud
That it will last the balance of your days!'
Roland replies, 'I hear proud foolishness.
Everyone knows that I care nought for threats.
This embassy requires a man of wisdom;
295 If the king wishes, I'll go in your place.'

XXI

But Ganelon answers, 'You'll not go for me. Aoi.
You're not my vassal, nor am I your lord.
King Charles commands that I should do his service;
I'll go to Saragoce to face Marsilie.
300 But I'll perform a little mischief there
Before my burning anger finds relief.'
When Roland heard this, he began to laugh. Aoi.

XXII

Ganelon sees his stepson Roland laugh;
His mood grows black; he almost bursts with rage,
305 And, very close to losing all control,
Says to the count, 'My love for you is gone.
Against me you have borne false witness here.
Just emperor, you see me here before you
Ready to carry out your own commands.'

XXIII

310 'I know that I must go to Saragoce; Aoi.
Whoever goes can nevermore return.
Recall I have your sister as my wife.
I have a son, no handsomer ever lived,
Named Baldewin,' said the count, 'who'll be a knight.
315 To him I leave my honours, rights and fiefs.
Watch o'er him well. I shall see him no more.'
The king replies, 'Your heart is tender indeed.
Since I command it, hither you must go.'

XXIV

Now says the king, 'Come forward, Ganelon, Aoi.
320 And so receive from me the glove and staff.
You've heard; the Franks have given this task to you.'
Ganelon replies, 'This all is Roland's doing;
While my life lasts, I'll show no love to him,
Nor Oliver, who's known as his companion,
325 Nor the twelve peers, because they love him so.
*Here I defy them, sire, within your sight.'
Then the king answers, 'You are full of anger.
You must leave now, since I command it so.'
'Though I may go, I go without protection; Aoi.
330 None had Basilie, nor his brother Basan.'

XXV

The emperor then hands him his right glove,
But Ganelon was there unwillingly
And, when he was to take it, let it fall.
The French say, 'God, what can this sign portend?
335 †Some great loss will befall us from this mission.'
'Lords, you'll hear news of it,' says Ganelon.

XXVI

'My lord,' says Ganelon, 'now give me leave.
Since go I must, I have no cause to tarry.'
The king declares, 'In Jesus' name and mine,'
340 With his right hand absolves and blesses him,
And then he hands him both the staff and brief.

XXVII

Count Ganelon retires to his own house.
There he begins to put on proper clothes,
The very best of all he could obtain.
345 He fixes spurs of gold upon his feet;
Murgleis, his sword, he buckles at his side
And mounts up on his war horse Tachebrun,
While Guinemer, his uncle, holds the stirrup.
Then might you have seen many a knight in tears,
350 †Saying, 'Alas that you were born for this!
Long have you held high status at the court!
Not a man there but called you 'noble vassal'!
But he who advocated you should go
Will not be safeguarded by Charlemagne.
355 Roland the count should not have thought of it,
For from great parentage is your descent.'
And then they beg, 'My lord, take us along!'
But Ganelon replies, 'Not so, please God!
Better I die alone than all these knights!
360 You'll make your way, my lords, back to sweet France.
On my behalf give greeting to my wife,
Also to Pinabel, my friend and peer;
And Baldewin, my own son whom you all know,
Help him, and hold him as your rightful lord.'
365 Then setting forth alone, he rides away. Aoi.

XXVIII

Ganelon rides up under an olive tree
And joins the Saracen ambassadors.
Blancandrin has been waiting with impatience.
They talk together shrewdly and with skill.
370 Says Blancandrin, 'A wondrous man is Charles,
Who conquered Puille and then all of Calabre;
Passing to England over the salty sea,
He levied Peter's pence for Rome's own use.
Why does he seek us out in our own land?'
375 Ganelon replies, 'Such is indeed his nature;
There'll never be a man to equal him.' Aoi.

XXIX

Says Blancandrin, 'The Franks are noble men,
But those dukes and those counts do him disservice,
Who give their lord such counsel and advice.
380 They trouble him and do great harm to others.'
Ganelon replies, 'I know of no such man;
Except for Roland who some day will pay.
Yesterday morn, while Charles sat in the shade,
His nephew came to him. Without his armour
385 He had gone foraging to Carcassonne.
He held a bright red apple in his hand,
"Take this, my lord," said Roland to his uncle,
"I bring you here the crowns of all the kings."
His very pride must be his own undoing,
390 For every day he seeks out mortal combat.
If someone could but kill him, we'd have peace.' Aoi.

XXX

Says Blancandrin, 'Violent and fierce is Roland.
He'd gladly bring all nations to surrender,
Challenge the sovereignty of every land.
395 With what force thinks he to accomplish this?'
*Ganelon responds, 'The French supply his strength.
They love him so, not one will ever fail him;
He puts such gold and silver in their hands,
So many mules and horses, silks, equipment;
400 The emperor himself has all he wants;
He'll conquer lands for him clear to the east.' Aoi.

XXXI

Ganelon and Blancandrin ride on until
Each to the other has pledged his word and sworn
That they will seek to have Count Roland killed.
405 Byways and roads they ride to Saragoce
Where underneath a yew tree they descend.
Under a pine tree's shade a faldstool stands,
Draped with a robe of Alexandrine silk,
Where sits the king who holds Spain in his power,
410 Some twenty thousand Saracens round about.
Not one man speaks or breathes a single word

For expectation of the impending news.
Behold now Ganelon and Blancandrin!

XXXII

Blancandrin comes before the king Marsilie,
415 Leading Count Ganelon forward by the hand,
Saying to the king, 'Mahomet's blessing on you!
Apollo's too, whose holy laws we keep!
We bore your message to King Charlemagne;
He lifted both his hands toward the heavens
420 And praised his God but made no other answer.
He sends you here one of his noble barons,
A man of France, a very powerful lord.
From him you'll hear if you'll have peace or not.'
Marsilie replies, 'Now let him speak; we'll listen.' AOI.

XXXIII

425 Now Ganelon has taken careful thought.
With wisdom and great skill he starts to speak
As one who knows just what he is about.
He says to the King, 'Blessings on you from God,
The Glorious One whom we should all adore!
430 The noble Charlemagne sends you his terms:
You must accept the holy Christian faith
And he will give you half of Spain in fief.
If you will not assent to this agreement,
You will be captured by his forces, bound,
435 And led off to his capital at Aix.
After a trial, you will be put to death.
There you will die in shame and degradation.'
The king Marsilie was very much wrought up;
He held a golden-feathered javelin
440 And would have struck had he not been prevented.
                                        AOI.
XXXIV

†King Marsilie's face is flushed with anger now;
Threateningly he shakes the javelin's shaft.
Seeing his rage, count Ganelon grasps his sword,
Draws it two fingers' breadth from out its sheath,
445 Saying to it, 'How beautiful and bright!

Long have I borne you in the court of kings!
The emperor of France will never say
That in a foreign land I died alone;
The noblest Saracens will pay you first!'
450 The pagans cry, 'Let us break up this fight!'

XXXV

The foremost Saracens then remonstrate
Until Marsilie has sat down on his throne:
The Caliph says, 'You do us only ill
In showing that you want to strike this Frank;
455 Your role should be to listen; hear him out.'
†Ganelon replies, 'This risk is but my duty.
I shall not fail, for all the gold God made
Nor yet for all the treasure in this land,
To say to him, as long as I have breath,
460 That Charles, the mighty, powerful king, calls him,
Through me he calls him, "mortal enemy"!'
The sable mantle draped around his shoulders,
Lined with a cloth of Alexandrine silk,
He throws to the ground; Blancandrin picks it up.
465 But Ganelon will not give up his sword;
In his right hand he holds the golden hilt.
The pagans cry, 'This is a noble lord!' Aoi.

XXXVI

Count Ganelon moves closer to the king,
Saying to him, 'Your sudden anger's wrong.
470 This is the message of King Charles of France,
That you accept the Christian law and faith
And as a fief he'll give you half of Spain.
His nephew Roland then will hold the rest;
A haughty partner you will have in him!
475 If you will not assent to this agreement,
He will lay siege to you in Saragoce.
He'll seize you forcefully and bind you fast;
Straight to his seat at Aix you will be led.
You'll ride no palfrey there, nor any charger;
480 No mule will you bestraddle on your way,
But you'll be thrown upon some old pack horse.

After a trial at Aix you'll lose your head.
Our emperor sends his terms in this his letter.'
With his right hand he gives it to the pagan.

XXXVII

485 King Marsilie's face was coloured high with anger.
He breaks the seal, throwing away the wax,
Looks at the letter and its written message.
'Charles bids me, he who holds France in his sway,
Recall the pain and anguish and the grief
490 I caused by killing Basan and Basilie
Whose heads I took on the hills above Haltilie.
He says that, if I wish to save my life,
I must send him my uncle the Caliph;
†There'll be no reconciliation else.'
495 *His son spoke up, in answer to Marsilie,
'Count Ganelon has spoken foolishly;
He's gone so far, it's not right he should live.
Give him to me and I'll work justice on him.'
When Ganelon hears, he brandishes his sword
500 And puts his back against a great pine's trunk.

XXXVIII

The king Marsilie has gone into a garden;
Along with him he takes his wisest men.
Among them is the white-haired Blancandrin
With Jurfaleu, King Marsilie's son and heir,
505 And the Caliph, Marsilie's uncle and friend.
Says Blancandrin, 'Now call the Frank before us;
He pledged me he would work to our advantage.'
The king agrees, 'Then lead him here yourself.'
Blancandrin takes the count by his right hand,
510 Leads him within the garden to the king.
There they discuss the means of wicked treason. AOI.

XXXIX

'Lord Ganelon,' the king addresses him,
'I acted rashly, thoughtlessly, just now,
Showing you anger enough to make me strike.

515 I pledge you with this gift of sable furs—
Their gold worth more than full five hundred pounds—
Tomorrow evening, fuller recompense.'
Ganelon replies, 'This I cannot refuse;
May it please God that he requite you well.' AOI.

XL

520 *Then speaks Marsilie, 'Believe me, Ganelon,
I feel an eagerness to be your friend.
I want to hear you speak of Charlemagne.
He is so old; his time is almost up;
I hear that he has passed two hundred years.
525 Without rest he has crossed so many lands,
Taken so many blows upon his shield,
Reduced so many kings to beggary;
When will he ever tire of making war?
Says Ganelon, 'Charles is not the man to tire.
530 There is no one who sees him, knows his mind,
But that he says the emperor is great.
I could not praise nor value him so high
But his nobility would surpass my words.
Who could recount his worth and reputation?
535 God has endowed him with such noble courage,
He'd die before forsaking all his barons.'

XLI

The pagan says, 'I have great cause to marvel
At Charlemagne, so white-haired and so old;
I do believe he's passed two hundred years.
540 Much has he travelled through so many lands,
Taken so many blows from lance and spear,
Reduced so many kings to beggary.
When will he ever tire of making war?'
'Never,' says Ganelon, 'while his nephew lives—
545 No vassal like him under heaven's vault.
Noble and brave his comrade Oliver
And the twelve peers whom King Charles holds so dear
Who form the van with twenty thousand knights.
Secure is Charles because he fears no man.' AOI.

XLII

550 Then says the Saracen, 'I marvel much
At Charlemagne, so hoary and white-haired,
For I am sure he's passed two hundred years.
He has gone conquering through so many lands,
From good sharp spears suffered so many blows,
555 Conquered in battle, killed such noble kings.
When will he ever tire of making war?'
'Never,' says Ganelon, 'while Roland lives;
No vassal like him from here to the east.
Noble and brave his comrade Oliver
560 And the twelve peers whom Charlemagne so loves;
They form the van with twenty thousand Franks.
Secure is Charles; he fears no living man.' Aoi.

XLIII

'My fair lord Ganelon,' says King Marsilie,
'I have an army, better you'll not see;
565 Four hundred thousand knights at my command.
Can I do battle with Charles and the French?'
Ganelon replies, 'No, never at this time.
You would sustain too great a loss of men.
Leave folly by and hold to wiser counsel.
570 Give to the emperor such wealth and goods
That there will be no Frank who will not marvel.
Contented by your twenty hostages,
The king will make his way back to sweet France
Leaving a force behind to guard his rear.
575 And there, I think, will be his nephew Roland
With Oliver, the noble courteous knight.
The counts are doomed, if I am but believed.
King Charles will see the downfall of his pride;
He will not seek to wage war on you more.' Aoi.

XLIV

580 'Lord Ganelon,' continues King Marsilie,
'In what way can I make an end of Roland?'
Ganelon replies, 'Indeed I'll tell you how.
Charles will be at Sizer, the easiest pass;

He will have placed his rearguard well behind.
585 Roland, his powerful nephew, will be there
And Oliver in whom he puts such trust;
Among their company, twenty thousand Franks;
Against them send a hundred thousand pagans!
Your men will first of all give battle to them;
590 The host of France will be cut up and battered.
But, since your men will suffer a great slaughter,
I say you must attack a second time.
Whate'er the outcome, Roland won't escape.
And thus you will have done a knightly deed
595 And never in your lifetime more have war. Aoi.

XLV

If someone could but see that Roland dies,
Then Charles would lose the right arm of his body.
Then would his dreaded hosts remain at home;
No more would Charles assemble such a force;
600 The land of France would henceforth know but peace.'
On hearing this, Marsilie embraces him,
Then sets about to open up his treasures. Aoi.

XLVI

'Now why discuss it further?' says Marsilie,
†'Uncertain counsel is a worthless thing;
605 So swear to me you will play Roland false.'
Ganelon responds, 'Let it be as you wish.'
On sacred relics in his sword Murgleis
He swore the treason and condemned himself. Aoi.

XLVII

A faldstool made of ivory stood near by
610 Where Marsilie had a book brought out before them:
*The law of Mahom and of Tervagant.
The Spanish Saracen then swore this oath:
If in the rearguard he can find count Roland,
With all his army he will fight with him;
615 If he prevails, Roland will surely die.
†Ganelon replies, 'Good fortune to your host.' Aoi.

XLVIII

There then appears a pagan Valdabrun,
†Who steps before the pagan king Marsilie
And, smiling brightly, says to Ganelon,
620 'Now take my sword, a better has no man,
*With over a thousand manguns in its hilt.
My lord, I give this to you out of friendship.
Now give us aid against the mighty Roland
That we may find him in King Charles' rearguard.'
625 'It shall be done,' replies Count Ganelon.
They kiss each other on the cheek and chin.

XLIX

Next there comes forth a pagan Climorin
Who, broadly smiling, says to Ganelon,
'Take here my helm; I never saw a better.
630 Now help our cause against the powerful Roland
In such a way as we may cause him shame.'
'It shall be done,' replies Count Ganelon.
They kiss each other on the mouth and cheek. Aoi.

L

Then comes upon the scene Queen Bramimonde,
635 Saying to the count, 'I love you greatly, sir,
Because my lord and all his men esteem you.
I send your lady wife two necklaces
Heavy with gold, jacinths and amethysts;
They are worth more than all the wealth of Rome.
640 Your emperor has never seen their like.'
He takes the jewels and stows them in his boot. Aoi.

LI

The king speaks to Malduit, his treasurer,
'Have you prepared the treasure for King Charles?'
And he replies, 'Yes, well enough, my lord:
645 Seven hundred camels bearing gold and silver
And twenty of earth's noblest hostages.' Aoi.

LII

Marsilie then puts his hand on Ganelon's shoulder
And says, 'You are a brave man and a wise.
By that same faith from which you hope salvation
650 Be careful not to change your view of us.
I plan to give you much of my own wealth:
Ten mules, all bearing purest Arab gold.
I'll do as much with every passing year.
Now take the keys to this wide city's gate;
655 Present this treasure from it to King Charles,
And then name Roland to the rearguard for me.
If I can find him at some mountain pass,
I shall engage him in a mortal battle.'
Ganelon replies, 'I tarry here too long.'
660 He mounts his horse and sets off on his way. Aoi.

LIII

The emperor draws ever nearer home.
Reaching the city Galne, he pauses there—
Count Roland took this town and broke its walls,
Since when it lay a hundred years deserted—
665 He is awaiting news of Ganelon
And of the tribute from the land of Spain.
At early dawn, just as the day awakes,
Comes Ganelon the count to the encampment. Aoi.

LIV

The emperor has risen very early;
670 Both mass and matins has the king attended.
He stands on the green grass before his tent;
With him are Roland and brave Oliver,
Duke Naimes and many others round about.
Ganelon comes up, the wicked, the forsworn,
675 And with great cunning now begins to speak,
Saying to the king, 'Blessings on you from God!
I bring you here the keys of Saragoce,
From whence I bear before you much great treasure
And twenty hostages—now guard them well!

680 The noble king Marsilie sends word to you
    That you not blame him for the Caliph's flight.
    My own eyes saw four hundred thousand men,
    Armed, wearing hauberks, some with helmets closed,
    Belted with swords, the hilts inlaid with gold,
685 Who led the Caliph off to the seashore.
    They flee Marsilie, because the law of Christ
    They will not willingly receive and keep.
    Yet ere these men had sailed four leagues away,
    Such storm and tempest overtook them all
690 That there they drowned; you will not see them more.
    Had he but lived, I would have brought him here.
    About the pagan king, you may be sure
    That you will not have seen this next month out
    Before he follows to your land of France,
595 There to receive that holy faith you hold
    And with hands joined your vassal to become;
    Thus he will hold the land of Spain from you.'
    Then speaks the king, 'May God be thanked for this!
    You have done well, much will it profit you.'
700 Among the host a thousand trumpets sound.
    The Franks break camp, load up their animals,
    And all set off upon the road to France. AOI.

                          LV
    King Charlemagne has now laid waste to Spain,
    Taken its castles and its cities ravaged.
705 Now the king says that he has done with war;
    The emperor rides off toward sweet France.
    Roland has fixed his standard on a staff
    And raised it heavenwards atop a hill.
    The Franks encamp throughout the countryside,
710 While pagans ride along the deepest valleys,
   *Wearing their hauberks, fully dressed for war.
    Their helmets laced, their swords are belted on,
    Shields hung about their necks, their lances decked.
    In a small wood atop the hills they stop,
715 Four hundred thousand strong, to wait the dawn.
    God, what a pity! The French are unaware. AOI.

LVI

So the day passes and the night grows dark.
Charles goes to sleep, the mighty emperor.
He dreams that he is at the pass at Size,
720 Holding his lance of ashwood in his hands.
Count Ganelon has seized it, torn it from him;
So violently he brandishes and shakes it
That splintered pieces fly towards the sky.
King Charles sleeps on; he does not rouse at all.

LVII

725 After this first, he dreamt another dream:
That he was in his chapel back at Aix.
†A wicked bear has bitten his right arm,
When from Ardennes he sees a leopard run
Which with great fierceness leaps directly at him.
730 A greyhound runs down from within Charles' hall
And, leaping with great speed, races to Charles.
First biting off the right ear of the bear,
It then attacks the leopard angrily.
The French stand round and watch the savage fight,
735 But none are certain which of them will win.
King Charles sleeps on and does not wake at all. Aoi.

LVIII

The darkness passes and the clear dawn comes;
Among the army, trumpets sound their blast;
The emperor rides proudly, nobly on.
740 'Now my lord barons,' says the emperor Charles,
'Behold the narrow defiles and the passes.
Appoint for me those who will guard the rear.'
'My stepson Roland!' answers Ganelon.
'You have no baron of such great distinction.'
745 On hearing this, the king looks at him fiercely
And says to him, 'You are a very devil!
A deadly hate has gotten into you!
Then who will ride before me in the van?'
'Oger of Denmark,' answers Ganelon,
750 'You have no baron who could do it better.'

LIX

Count Roland, when he heard himself appointed, AOI.
In courteous, knightly manner made reply:
'My lord stepfather, I have cause to love you,
Since you've appointed me to the rearguard.
755 Charles who rules France will not lose by this move,
In my opinion, palfrey or war horse,
Nor any mule he might wish to bestride:
Nor even a simple pack horse will he lose,
But that it will be paid for by the sword.'
760 Ganelon replies, 'You speak the truth, I know.' AOI.

LX

*When Roland heard that he would guard the rear,
With anger he replied to his stepfather,
'Foul wretch! Base fellow of ignoble line!
You thought that this time I would drop the glove
765 Just as you did the staff before the king?' AOI.

LXI

'Just emperor,' said Roland, noble and brave,
'Give me the bow that you hold in your hand.
I do not think that any will reproach
My dropping it as did Count Ganelon
770 From his right hand when he received the staff.'
The emperor just sits with his head bowed;
He strokes his beard and twists at his moustache.
He cannot help that tears come to his eyes.

LXII

Whereat before the council steps Duke Naimes—
775 No better vassal ever stood in court—
And says to the king, 'You've heard what has gone on;
This time it is Count Roland who is angry.
But the rearguard has been assigned to him;
No baron now can alter the decision.
780 Hand him the bow that you have ever drawn
And find him men who best can give him aid.'
Charles yields the bow and Roland takes it up.

LXIII

The emperor addresses then his nephew,
'My noble nephew, know I speak in earnest.
785　Half of my army I shall leave with you.
But keep them with you, you will be secure.'
The count replies, 'I never shall do that!
May God destroy me if I soil my name!
I shall keep twenty thousand valiant Franks.
790　Go through the passes certain of your safety
And stand in fear of no man while I live!'

LXIV

Roland the count has mounted on his charger.
His comrade Oliver comes to his side.
Gerin comes too, and noble Count Gerer;
795　Otes follows him along with Berenger,
And then Astor and Anseïs the proud,
With them the old Girart de Rossillon,
Gaifier who is a noble, powerful duke.
Says the archbishop, 'By my head, I'll go!'
800　'And I with you!' replies the count Gualter,
'As Roland's vassal, I shall never fail him.'
Among them, they choose twenty thousand knights.
　　　　　　　　　　　　　　　　　　AOI.

LXV

Count Roland calls out to Gualter del Hum,
'Select a thousand Franks from our own France
805　And occupy the defiles and the hills
Lest the emperor should lose a single man.'
Gualter replies, 'For you I'll do my best,'
And with a thousand men of France their land
Deploys patrols among the hills and vales.
810　He will not come down, even for bad news,
Before some seven hundred swords be drawn.
King Almaris, the ruler of Belferne,
Will give him battle on the awful day.

LXVI

Lofty the hills, the valleys deep in shadow,
815　Dark the high rocks, the defiles ominous.

The French have spent the day in painful toil,
Their din in passing heard for fifteen leagues.
Before they reach the borders of their land,
They catch sight of Charles' land of Gascony.
820 Then they recall their own domains and fiefs,
Their virgin daughters and their noble wives.
Not one of them but sheds a tear for love.
Above all others Charles is full of anguish;
He's left his nephew at the pass to Spain;
825 Assailed by tender thoughts, he can but weep. Aoi.

LXVII

The twelve peers have been left behind in Spain
Accompanied by twenty thousand Franks;
Not one is timorous or afraid to die.
The emperor is moving home toward France;
830 Under his cloak he hides his countenance.
Duke Naimes, who rides along beside the king,
Asks of his lord, 'What weighs upon your mind?'
Charles answers, 'You do ill to ask me that.
I grieve so much, I cannot but lament.
835 Our France will be destroyed by Ganelon.
Last night there came to me an angel's vision
Where in my very hands he broke my lance
Who sent my nephew to command the rear.
I have left Roland on a foreign soil.
840 God! If I lose him now I'll have no other.' Aoi.

LXVIII

Now Charlemagne cannot restrain his tears.
A hundred thousand Franks commiserate
With him and share a dreadful fear for Roland.
The evil Ganelon has played him false
845 And for this from the pagan king received
Rich gifts of gold and silver, silken cloth,
Both mules and horses, camels and lions too!
Meanwhile, Marsilie sends for the lords of Spain,
*Counts and viscounts, his dukes and almaçurs,
850 His emirs and the sons of lesser lords,

Four hundred thousand in three days assembled.
He has his drums beat loud in Saragoce;
They raise Mahomet to the highest tower;
No pagan there but prays and worships him.
855 United in the rivalry of zeal,
They ride out over plain and hill and vale
Until they sight the standards of the French.
The rearguard of the twelve peers and companions,
Will never fail to give them battle here.

LXIX

860 The nephew of Marsilie rode to the fore
Astride a mule he urged on with his staff,
Addressed his uncle, laughing all the while,
'My lord the king, I have served you so long,
Much pain and suffering have I undergone
865 And in the field so many battles won;
Grant me one right: to strike at Roland first.
I'll kill him with my own sharp-pointed spear.
Will Mahomet but give me his protection,
I shall redeem the conquered lands of Spain
870 South from the mountain pass to Durestant.
Charles will grow tired; his Franks will then give up.
Through all your life you'll never more have war.'
Assenting, King Marsilie gives him the glove.

LXX

The nephew holds the glove clutched in his fist
875 And proudly, boldly, speaks to King Marsilie,
'Fair lord and king, you've given me one great boon.
Now choose for me among your barons twelve
With whom I'll fight against the twelve companions.'
The first to volunteer is Falsaron—
880 He was a brother of the king Marsilie—
'My lord, my nephew, you and I shall go
And in great earnest press this battle hotly.
As for the rearguard of Charles' mighty host,
It is decreed that we shall kill them all.' Aoi.

LXXI

885 King Corsalis rides up to join them now;
He is a Berber, evil, full of craft.
He speaks to them as a good vassal should;
He would not be a coward for God's gold.
Comes spurring up Malprimis de Brigant—
890 Fleeter of foot is he than any horse—
And shouts in a loud voice before Marsilie,
'Now I myself shall go to Rencesvals;
If I find Roland, naught can save his life.'

LXXII

Next there appears the emir of Balaguer,
895 Noble of build, open and proud of mien.
Since the first day he mounted on a horse,
He has grown haughty in the use of arms.
Renowned is he for many valorous deeds.
If Christian, he would be a perfect knight.
900 Before Marsilie he cries with a loud voice,
'I too shall make my way to Rencesvals.
If I find Roland there, his death is sealed,
With Oliver and all of the twelve peers.
The French will die disgraced, in ignominy.
905 This Charlemagne is old and doddering;
He'll soon be tired of waging war on us.
Spain will be ever ours in peace and quiet.'
The king Marsilie thanked him most heartily. Aoi.

LXXIII

Then comes an almaçur of Moriane,
910 No man more wicked in the land of Spain.
He made his boast before the king Marsilie:
'To Rencesvals I'll lead my company
Of twenty thousand men with lance and spear.
If I find Roland, I assure his death.
915 There'll never be a day Charles will not mourn.' Aoi.

LXXIV

There then rides up Turgis de Turteluse.
He is a count; he holds and rules that town.
To slaughter Christians is his single aim.

He joins the other lords before Marsilie
920 And says to him, 'Lord, never show dismay!
Mahomet's stronger than the Roman Peter;
If you serve him, we'll have the battle honours.
At Rencesvals, I shall attack this Roland;
He will find none to shield him there from death.
925 See here my sword which is both strong and long!
I'll match it on the field with Durendal;
You will hear far and wide who won the day.
The French will die if they fight with us now.
Old Charlemagne will suffer grief and shame
930 And never more on this earth wear his crown.'

LXXV

From another side comes riding Escremiz;
He is a Saracen, lord of Valterne.
He shouts out in the crowd before Marsilie,
'At Rencesvals, I shall lay low their pride.
935 If I find Roland, he will lose his head
And Oliver who captains all the rest;
The twelve peers likewise all are doomed to die.
The French will die and France will be bereft;
King Charlemagne will want for vassals then.' Aoi.

LXXVI

940 The pagan Esturgan comes riding up,
His comrade Estramariz at his side,
Both of them wicked, traitorous, knavish, false.
Marsilie says to them, 'Lords, come here before me!
Taking the mountain passes, will you go
945 To Rencesvals and lead my army there.'
The two reply, 'As you command, my lord!
We shall attack both Oliver and Roland
And the twelve peers shall have no shield from death.
Our swords are of the best and very sharp
950 And we shall make them crimson with fresh blood.
The French will die; Charles will be full of grief.
We'll put into your hands the whole of France.
Come with us, sire! You'll see it for yourself.
We'll hand the very emperor to you!'

LXXVII

955 Margariz de Sebilie comes riding fast.
His lands extend as far as Cazmarine.
His handsomeness wins all the women to him;
Not one sees him whose face does not light up
Or, glancing at him, can repress a smile.
960 No other pagan shows such chivalry.
Entering the crowd, he shouts above the others,
And cries to the king, 'Sire, do not be dismayed!
At Rencesvals, I'll put an end to Roland,
And Oliver will not escape alive;
965 The twelve French peers are doomed to bloody
      slaughter.
See here my sword, hilted in solid gold,
A gift sent me by the emir of Primes.
I promise you to dip it in red blood.
The French will die and France be brought to shame.
970 As for old Charles, his beard all hoary white,
There'll be no day he'll not know grief and rage.
Within a year we shall have taken France;
We'll lie at ease within Saint Denis' walls.'
The pagan king bows deeply to this lord.

LXXVIII

975 And last rides up Chernuble de Munigre,
His hair so long it sweeps right to the ground.
To amuse himself, he'll carry greater weight
Than four pack mules could bear upon their backs.
He claims that in the land from which he comes
980 No sun can shine, nor wheat can ever grow;
There falls no rain, nor gathers any dew;
There is no stone nor rock that is not black.
Some say it is the land where devils dwell.
Chernuble speaks, 'I've girded on my sword.
985 At Rencesvals I'll keep it crimson-stained.
If I should find brave Roland in my path
And not attack, I'll not deserve your trust.
With my own sword I shall win Durendal.
The French will die and France will be bereft.'
990 Upon these words the pagan peers assemble,

Lead out a hundred thousand Saracens,
All hastening and eager for the fight.
Within a grove of pines, they arm themselves.

LXXIX

The pagans don their Saracen coats of mail,
995 Most of them made of triple-layered chain.
They lace good helmets made at Saragoce,
Gird on their swords of good steel from Vienne.
They all have fine shields and Valencian spears;
*All crimson, blue and white their gonfanons.
1000 They leave the palfreys and the mules behind
And, mounting chargers, ride in close array.
The day is fair, the sunshine bright and clear;
Equipment shines and flashes in the light;
A thousand trumpets now enhance the scene.
1005 Great is their noise and the French hear it well.
Says Oliver, 'My lord comrade, I think
A mighty battle they will give us now.'
Roland replies, 'May God grant us the field!
Here we must stand in duty to our king:
1010 A man should suffer greatly for his lord,
Put up with heat, withstand the bitter cold
And, as his duty, lose both hide and hair.
Let now each man prepare to strike great blows
So that no bad report of us be sung!
1015 The pagan cause is wrong, the Christian right!
And no unworthy model will I be!' Aoi.

LXXX

Oliver, from atop a lofty hill
Looks to the right down through a grassy vale
And sees the pagan army on the march;
1020 This he reports to Roland his companion.
'Over towards Spain I see the flash of arms,
The shining coats of mail, the gleaming helms;
They will spread woe, distress, among our Franks.
The forsworn traitor Ganelon knew this
1025 Who placed our names before the emperor.'

'Be silent, Oliver,' replies the count.
'Against my stepfather I'll hear no charge.'

LXXXI

Count Oliver has gone atop a hill
From where he can observe the fields of Spain
1030 And all the Saracens assembled there.
There shine those helmets all bedecked with gold,
†The bucklers and the hauberks damascened,
The lances with their gonfanons attached.
He cannot even estimate divisions,
1035 So numerous they, he cannot count their number.
Now Oliver himself is much alarmed;
As quickly as he can, rides down the hill,
Comes to the Franks and gives a full report.

LXXXII

Says Oliver, 'I have seen pagans here
1040 In numbers such as none e'er saw on earth:
A hundred thousand in the van with shields,
Their helmets laced secure, in shining mail,
The lances shine, their wooden shafts upraised.
You'll have a battle such as never was.
1045 My lords of France, may you have strength from God!
Stand firm in the field, lest we be overcome!'
The French reply, 'May God curse those who flee!
None here for fear of death will fail you now.' Aoi.

LXXXIII

Says Oliver, 'The pagans are in force,
1050 While of our Franks it seems there are too few.
Therefore, companion Roland, sound your horn!
King Charles will hear, the army will turn back.'
Roland replies, 'That would be mad, insane!
For I would lose renown throughout sweet France.
1055 Instead, I'll strike great blows with Durendal,
Bloody the blade up to the golden hilt.
Luckless the day they rode out to this pass.
I promise you, all are condemned to die.' Aoi.

LXXXIV

'Roland, my comrade, sound the ivory horn!
1060 For Charles will hear it and turn back his host.
The king will bring his nobles to our aid.'
Roland replies, 'May the Lord God forbid
That through my fault my family suffer shame
Or that dear France fall into disrepute.
1065 Rather, I'll strike great blows with Durendal,
My own good sword which I have girded on.
You'll see the whole blade red with pagan blood.
Ill-starred this massing of the Saracens;
I promise you, all are as good as dead.' Aoi.

LXXXV

1070 *'Companion Roland, sound your olifant
And Charles will hear it, marching through the pass.
I promise you, the Franks will then return.'
'May God forbid,' Roland replies to him,
'That it be claimed by any man alive
1075 I blew the horn for fear of Saracens!
My family shall not suffer that reproach!
When I am in the battle's bloody heart,
*I'll strike more blows than any man can count.
Durendal's blade you'll see all red with blood.
1080 The French are of the best, so will they fight.
The men of Spain will find no shield from death.'

LXXXVI

†Says Oliver, 'The horn will bring no shame.
With my own eyes I've seen the Saracens,
The hills and mountains covered with their host,
1085 The hillsides and the plains to the horizon.
Vast is the army of this foreign land,
And we are but a little company.'
Roland replies, 'That makes my zeal redouble.
May God forbid, and all His heavenly host,
1090 That France should lose her honour through my fault.
I'll die before I'll be sought out by shame.
†It is by fighting that we win Charles' love.'

LXXXVII

Heroic Roland and wise Oliver,
Each a great vassal of prodigious courage.
1095 Since they have mounted horses, taken arms,
Neither will shun the battle, fleeing death;
The counts are noble, lofty are their words.
In zealous wrath the wicked pagans ride.
Says Oliver, 'See in what strength they come!
1100 They're close to us but Charles is far away.
You did not deign to sound the olifant;
Were the king here, our loss were not so great.
But glance up there towards the pass to Spain
And you will see the reaguard's melancholy;
1105 Who fights this day will never fight another.'
Roland replies, 'Speak no outrage to honour!
Woe to the heart turned coward in the breast!
We'll stand in our positions on this spot,
And we shall strike the blows and wield the swords.'
                                              Aoi.

LXXXVIII

1110 When Roland sees the battle near at hand,
His courage swells, more fierce than lion or leopard.
He calls the French and shouts to Oliver,
'My lord companion, friend, hold back such words!
The emperor who left these French with us
1115 —His own selection of some twenty thousand—
Was well assured no coward was among them.
A man should suffer greatly for his lord,
Endure both biting cold and sweltering heat
And sacrifice for him both flesh and blood.
1120 Strike with your lance as I with Durendal,
My own good sword, a present from the king.
If I die here, whoever has it next
†May say it was a noble vassal's sword.'

LXXXIX

Archbishop Turpin, far across the field,
1125 Spurs on his horse and gallops up a hill.
He calls the French and speaks these words to them:

'Barons, my lords, King Charles has left us here.
We should die well and nobly for our king.
Offer your help to succour Christendom!
1130 You will have battle; be quite sure of that;
With your own eyes you saw the Saracens.
Confess your sins and ask the grace of God.
I shall absolve you to protect your souls.
If you die here, you will be holy martyrs.
1135 You will have seats in highest paradise.'
The French dismount and kneel upon the ground;
In God's name the archbishop blesses them
And for their penance orders them to fight.

XC

The French lift up their heads, get to their feet;
1140 They are absolved and quit of all their sins;
The archbishop has blessed them in God's name.
Then, on their swift war horses mounted up,
Wearing the armour that befits their rank,
†They form their lines, make ready for the fight.
1145 Count Roland calls out then to Oliver:
'My lord companion, you knew well indeed
Ganelon has betrayed us one and all.
He's taken gold and coin and riches for it;
The emperor must take revenge for us.
1150 The king Marsilie has bargained for our lives,
But he will have to pay the bill with swords.' Aoi.

XCI

Down through the Spanish passes Roland rides
Astride his charger, the swift Veillantif,
Wearing his armour, splendidly arrayed.
1155 See how he flourishes his lance on high,
The shining point turned upward towards the sky,
And at the top a pure white battle flag,
†Whose golden streamers flutter to his hands;
Noble his form, his face is laughing, bright.
1160 His comrade Oliver rides close behind.
The French call him protector, champion;

Towards the pagans, Roland's gaze is proud;
Humble and fond each glance back at the French.
He speaks a final gallant, knightly word:
1165†'My lords and barons, slowly, keep in line!
These pagans seek, unknowing, their own death.
Today we'll win a booty of such worth
No king of France has ever had its peer.'
The armies, at these words, prepare to charge. AOI.

XCII

1170 Count Oliver asserts, 'I'll speak no more.
You did not deign to sound the olifant
And so you will have no help from King Charles.
He knows not of our plight; he bears no blame,
Nor do those men behind us on the slopes.
1175 Now ride, my lords, with all the speed you can!
And hold your ground, brave barons, in the field!
I pray you, in the name of God, take care
To strike great blows and give back all you take.
Today let's not forget Charles' battle cry!'
1180 In answer to his words the French cry out;
*Whoever that day heard them shout 'Montjoie!'
Recalled their valour ever afterwards.
And ride they did. God! with what fearsome zeal
They spurred ahead, each trying to gain the fore.
1185†They sped towards the combat, duty bound.
The Saracens, courageous, fear them not.
Behold the Franks and pagans clash in war!

XCIII

The nephew of Marsilie, named Aëlroth,
Is first to ride in front of all their host.
1190 He calls insulting slogans to the French:
'Villainous French, you'll fight with us today.
He who was to protect you, sold you out.
The king's a fool who left you in the pass.
Today your sweet France will lose all its fame
1195 And Charlemagne the right arm of his body!'

When Roland hears him, God! his grief is such
He spurs his horse and headlong lets him run,
Seeking to strike the pagan as he can,
He breaks his shield and rips his hauberk open,
1200 Pierces his chest, crushing the ribs and bones,
Tearing his spine loose all along his back,
And with his lance he drives out soul from body.
He spits him cleanly, sends him toppling;
†With outstretched spear, he strikes him from his horse
1205 And in two halves he breaks the pagan's neck.
Roland cannot refrain from speaking thus:
'Less than ignoble wretch! Charles is not mad,
Nor did he ever love the path of treason.
It was a noble act to leave us here
1210 And sweet France will not lose her fame today.
Fight on now, Franks, the day's first blow is ours!
Ours is the right, these infidels' the wrong!'

XCIV

A pagan duke was there, named Falsaron.
He was the brother of the king Marsilie
1215 And ruled the lands of Dathan, Abirun.
'Neath heaven's arch lived no more thorough pagan:
His forehead was so broad between his eyes.
Its measure must have been a good half foot.
Seeing his nephew dead, his grief is great:
1120 He rides out from the crowd and offers battle;
Shouting aloud the pagan battle cry,
Mockingly he calls insults to the French:
'Today your sweet France loses all her glory!'
Oliver hears; his anger is so great,
1225 Into his horse he digs his golden spurs
And rides out, noble man, to strike him down.
He rends his shield and tears his hauberk off;
Into his body rams the pennant tails
As with his lance he strikes him from the saddle.
1230 Then, looking down to where the villain lies,
He speaks to him in bold and warlike words:
'You wretch, I am not hindered by your threats.

Fight on now, Franks! The victory shall be ours!'
He shouts 'Montjoie!' the battle cry of Charles. Aoi.

XCV

1235 Another pagan named King Corsalis
—A Berber from a strange and foreign land—
Calls out then to the other Saracens:
'This is a battle we shall surely win;
The number of the French is very small.
1240 Those few before us here we may hold cheap,
For not a single one will Charles protect.
This is the day when they are doomed to die.'
Archbishop Turpin hears this pagan's words—
'Neath heaven no other man he hated so.
1245 Urging his horse with spurs of purest gold,
He rides to strike him down with all his might.
Breaking the shield and tearing through the mail,
Right through this king he rams his mighty lance.
Spitting him well, he sends him reeling, dead.
1250 His lance outstretched, he kills him in full flight.
Then, looking back to where the pagan lies,
He cannot help but speak these words to him:
'Foul infidel, your words are now proved wrong;
For Charles my lord is ever our protector;
1255 Our men of France have no desire to flee;
We'll lay all your companions to their rest.
Be sure of this, your lot today is death.
Fight on now, Franks, let none forget his duty!
This first blow is for us, thanks be to God!'
1260 He shouts 'Montjoie!' to rally all the field.

XCVI

Gerin attacks Malprimis de Brigant
*Whose shield, though strong, proves not a denier's
worth.
The crystal boss is shattered with one blow,
The one half of it flying to the ground.
1265 Straight through the hauberk, baring all the flesh,
Into the body Gerin thrusts his lance.
The pagan tumbles off, all in a heap
And Satan carries off his soul to hell. Aoi.

XCVII

Gerer his comrade strikes the amurafle;
1270 Smashing his shield, he breaks the chains of mail;
Into his middle stabs the heavy lance,
Thrusting so hard, he runs him cleanly through
And stretches him out dead upon the field.
Cries Oliver, 'Our fight is noble indeed!'

XCVIII

1275 Duke Sansun then attacks the almaçur,
Splitting his shield all decked with flowers and gold.
A good hauberk is no defence for him;
He stabs him in the liver, heart and lungs,
Striking him dead whomever it may grieve.
1280 Archbishop Turpin cries, 'A noble blow!'

XCIX

Lord Anseïs then gives his horse full rein
And rides to strike Turgis de Turteluse.
He splits his shield above the golden boss,
Tears through the hauberk's double chains of mail
1285 And stabs him with the point of his stout lance.
He strikes so well, the steel goes in and through.
With outstretched lance, he slays him on the field.
Count Roland shouts, 'That was a worthy blow!'

C

Then Engeler the Gascon from Bordeaux
1290 Sets spur to horse, abandons rein and rides
To fight against Escremiz de Valterne.
Shattering the shield around the pagan's neck,
Tearing the chain mail round his head and chin,
He strikes full in the middle of his chest;
1295 With lance outstretched, he knocks him from the
    saddle.
Says Engeler, 'Now you have met your death.' AOI.

CI

Then Gualter strikes the pagan Esturgan
Right at the upper edge of his bright shield,

Splitting its painted quarters, red and white.
1300 Ripping the hauberk right along its seam,
He drives the sharpened lance point through his flesh,
Striking him dead from his own swift war horse.
Gualter cries out, 'No man will save you now!'

CII

Then Berenger attacks Estramariz;
1305 He breaks his shield and tears his hauberk through.
He spits him through the body with his lance
And leaves his corpse amidst the Saracen dead.
Of the twelve pagan peers, ten have been killed;
Upon the field, but two remain alive;
1310 Their names: Chernuble and Count Margariz.

CIII

Margariz is a very valiant knight,
Handsome and strong and swift and quick in fight.
He spurs his horse, attacking Oliver.
Breaking the golden boss of the Frank's shield,
1315 He runs his lance close in along his side.
But God insures he does not wound him there.
The wood shaft shatters, does not strike him down,
And Margariz, unhindered, rides on through
And sounds his horn to rally all his men.

CIV

1320 Widespread and fearful is the battle now.
Count Roland does not hang back from the fight,
Strikes with his lance, long as the wood endures.
In fifteen blows the shaft is splintered, gone.
So, drawing naked steel, good Durendal,
1325 He spurs his horse and rides to attack Chernuble.
Striking his helmet set with shining stones,
He splits his coif and so on through his hair,
Striking down twixt the eyes and through the face,
Down through the shining hauberk's close-knit mail,
1330 On through the body, downward through the crotch,
Into the saddle bright with beaten gold,

Until within the horse the blade is stopped.
It splits the pagan's spine, seeking no joint,
And lays him dead there on the thick field grass.
1335 Then Roland speaks, 'Woe that you came this way,
For from Mahomet you will have no help.
Such miscreants shall never win this field.'

CV

Count Roland rides across the battlefield;
The well-honed Durendal is in his hand;
1340 He slaughters many of the Saracens.
See how he piles them one atop the other,
The bright blood spread about on every hand!
Bloody his hauberk, bloody both his arms,
The neck and shoulders of his good war horse.
1345 Nor yet is Oliver slow to attack;
The twelve French peers deserve no blame today;
The Franks continue fighting hand to hand;
Some pagans faint from wounds and others die.
Archbishop Turpin cries, 'God bless our band!'
1350 He shouts 'Montjoie!', the battle cry of Charles. Aoi.

CVI

Count Oliver goes riding through the fray,
His lance is broken, but the shaft remains.
With this he attacks the Saracen Malun;
He breaks the pagan's golden, flowered shield
1355 And knocks his two eyes straight out of his head;
The brains fall out and lie there at his feet.
He lays him mid his seven hundred dead
And then he slays Turgis and Esturguz.
The lance shaft splits and shatters to the grip.
1360†Roland calls out, 'Companion, what is this?
I have no use for clubs in such a battle.
This is the field where iron and steel prove true.
Where is your sword which men all call Halteclere?
Crystal its pommel, gold its two cross guards.'
1365 'I could not draw it,' Oliver replies,
'Great was my need to strike a blow in haste.' Aoi.

CVII

Lord Oliver has drawn his good sword now,
As Roland his companion begged him to,
And shown him its great worth like a good knight.
1370 He sets upon Justin de Valferrée
And cleanly cleaves his head right down the middle,
Slicing the body and the shining mail,
Right through the golden-ornamented saddle
Until he splits the backbone of the horse.
1375 He strikes the pagan dead there in the field.
Roland calls out, 'I recognize a brother.
For such blows does the emperor love us dear.'
Then on all sides is heard the cry 'Montjoie!' AOI.

CVIII

The count Gerin astride his horse Sorel,
1380 And his companion Gerer on Passecerf,
Let go their reins and eagerly both spur
And strike a Saracen named Timozel,
One on the hauberk, the other on the shield.
They break their lances off within his body
1385 And lay him dead amid the fallow field.
I have not heard it told and cannot say
*Which of the two was quicker in the deed.
The son of Burel, named Esperveres,
He was killed by Engeler of Bordeaux.
1390 Archbishop Turpin then killed Siglorel,
The enchanter who had visited in hell;
Jupiter led him there by sorcery.
Turpin calls out, 'This one was marked for death.'
Roland replies, 'The wretch has met his fate.
1395 My brother Oliver, I love such blows.'

CIX

The battle meanwhile grows more stubborn still,
Both Franks and pagans striking wondrous blows,
Attackers and defenders intermingled.
How many lances broken, bloody now!
1400 How many gonfanons and flags are torn!
How many French have spent their youth this day!

They'll see no more their mothers nor their wives,
Nor yet the French who await them at the pass. Aoi.

CX

The emperor Charles weeps for them and laments.
1405 What use is this? They'll have no help from him.
Ganelon served him ill that fatal day
On which, at Saragoce, he sold Charles' men.
He died for that and lost his life and limbs;
The trial at Aix condemned him to be hanged
1410 Along with thirty of his relatives
Who had no expectation they would die. Aoi.

CXI

The battle now is grievous, terrible;
Roland and Oliver fight hard and well,
Archbishop Turpin strikes unnumbered blows,
1415 The twelve French peers do not restrain their arms,
The men of France press the attack together.
The pagans die in hundreds and in thousands,
Who does not flee can find no shield from death;
Will he or not, there he will lose his life.
1420 The French will lose their finest knights this day;
They'll see no more their fathers or their families,
Nor Charlemagne who at the pass awaits.
In France there breaks a wondrous, fearful storm,
A tempest full of thunder and of wind,
1425 With sheets of rain and hail unprecedented;
The bolts of lightning fall on every hand
And even earthquakes rock and shake the land.
From Mont Saint Michel all the way to Seinz,
From Besançon to Guitsand in the north,
1430 There is no house but whose walls crack and split.
The shadows gather thick at highest noon,
All darkness, save where lightning rends the sky.
Each man who sees the storm is filled with dread
And many say, 'This is the Judgement Day.
1435 The ending of the world is near at hand.'
They do not know that what they say is wrong;
This is the mourning for the death of Roland.

CXII

The French have fought with vigour and great heart;
Pagans have died in swarms a thousand strong,
1440 Two thousand of their hundred thousand left.
Archbishop Turpin says, 'Our men are brave.
No man on earth had ever better ones.
Now is it written in the song of France,
Our emperor had vassals of the best.'
1445 Throughout the field they ride, seeking their own,
Weeping the tears of grief and tenderness
For brothers in allegiance and in blood.
†King Marsilie is upon them with his host. Aoi.

CXIII

Along a valley floor King Marsilie rides
1450 With the great army that he had assembled;
Twenty divisions can the pagan count,
With gold and jewels their helmets shining bright
Their shields and hauberks worked in damascene.
Some seven thousand trumpets sound the charge;
1455 The blast is heard for many miles around.
Says Roland, 'Oliver, companion, friend,
The wicked Ganelon has sworn our death.
This treason cannot longer be concealed.
The emperor will exact awful revenge.
1460 Today we'll fight a battle, long and hard;
No man has ever seen so fierce a one.
I shall attack with Durendal, my sword
And you, my lord companion, with Halteclere.
We've borne these weapons in so many fields
1465 And won so many battles with their blades.
Of them shall no unworthy song be sung!' Aoi.

CXIV

Now Marsilie sees the slaughter of his men
And has his horns and trumpets sound the charge.
Forward he rides with his assembled host.

1470 In front there rides a Saracen, Abisme,
　　No man more wicked in that company;
　　His character is evil, vile his crimes;
　　He has no trust in God, Saint Mary's Son.
　　His visage is as black as melted pitch.
1475 More love had he for treason and for murder
　　Than he could feel for all Galicia's gold.
　　No man had ever seen him sport or laugh.
　　A man of courage, of great recklessness,
　　He was the favourite of the king Marsilie
1480 Whose dragon staff he bore to call his men.
　　The archbishop will bear him naught but hatred.
　　Seeing the pagan, Turpin longs to strike
　　And quietly he murmurs to himself,
　　'This Saracen appears a great heretic;
1485 The best course is for me to go and slay him.
　　*I have no love for cowards or their ways.' Aoi.

CXV

　　The archbishop is first to join the battle,
　　Astride the horse he'd taken from Grossaille
　　—That was a king he slew in Denmark once—
1490 A swift horse this and very fleet of foot,
　　Its leg was slender and its hoof well arched,
　　Short in the thigh and powerful in the croup,
　　Long in the ribs and high along the back,
　　A pure white tail he bore, a golden mane,
1495 Small ears upon his golden-coloured head;
　　There was no beast that might compare with him.
　　Archbishop Turpin spurs courageously,
　　Determined to attack this pagan lord,
　　And strike a wondrous blow upon his shield
1500 Bedecked with topaz and with amethyst,
　　With burning carbuncles and precious stones.
　　†A devil gave it him at Val Metas,
　　A present from the amiral Galafes.
　　Turpin strikes home and does not spare the shield;
1505 After his blow, it's not worth a denier.
　　He cuts him through from one side to the other,

Striking him dead amid the fallow field.
The French exclaim, 'A brave, courageous act!
*The archbishop's crozier has a mighty power!'

CXVI

1510 The French now realize the pagan numbers;
On every side they fill the battlefield.
The French cry out to Oliver and Roland
To ask protection from them and the peers.
Archbishop Turpin tells the French his thoughts:
1515 'My lords, yield not to weakness nor to fear!
In God's own name I beg you not to flee,
Lest noble men sing wicked songs of you.
Better by far that we should die in battle!
This we are promised: here and now we die.
1520 Not one of us shall live beyond this day.
But one thing I can pledge and guarantee:
That paradise lies open to your souls;
You will have seats among the Innocents.'
On hearing this, the French rejoice again;
1525 Not one of them but cries aloud 'Montjoie!' Aoi.

CXVII

There was a Saracen from Saragoce
—Half of that city could he call his own—
Named Climorin. He had no chivalry.
*He took the oath sworn by Count Ganelon,
1530 Then out of friendship kissed him on the mouth,
Gave him his helmet and his carbuncle.
He made the claim, he would dishonour France
And take the emperor's crown from off his head.
He sits upon his horse called Barbamusche—
1535 Faster it was than sparrow-hawk or swallow—
He spurs it well and lets go of the reins,
Attacking Engeler of Gascony,
Whom neither shield nor hauberk can protect.
The pagan thrusts the lance point in his body,
1540 Striking him squarely, thrusts the iron through.
With outstretched lance, he knocks him over dead.

Climorin shouts, 'These men are best destroyed!
*Press the attack now, pagans; break their ranks!'
The French lament, 'We mourn this noble man.' Aoi.

CXVIII

1545 Count Roland then calls out to Oliver,
'My lord companion, Engeler is dead.
We had no better nor more valiant knight.'
The count replies, 'God grant I may avenge him!'
He set his spurs of pure gold to his horse
1550 And, holding Halteclere's bloody steel on high,
Rides out and strikes the pagan with great force.
Oliver strikes his blow; Climorin falls;
The devil carries off his pagan soul.
Count Oliver then slays Duke Alphaien,
1555 Escababi is next to lose his head,
Then Oliver unhorses seven Arabs
Who cease to be of any use for war.
Roland observes, 'My comrade is now angry.
Compared to me, he acts most valiantly.
1560 For such blows does King Charles hold us most dear.'
In a loud voice he shouts, 'Attack, lord knights!' Aoi.

CXIX

The pagan Valdabrun comes riding up;
He was raised from a child by King Marsilie.
Upon the sea he has four hundred ships;
1565 No ship-master but takes his rank from him.
He took Jerusalem by treachery
And desecrated Solomon's own temple,
Killing the patriarch before the fonts.
He also took the oath of Ganelon,
1570 Gave him the sword, a thousand golden coins.
He sits upon a horse called Gramimund,
Far faster than a falcon is this mount.
With sharpened spurs he urges him to run
And rides to strike the noble Duke Sansun.
1575 He smashes both his shield and hauberk too,
Ramming his gonfanon into his body.

With outstretched lance, he knocks him from the saddle.
'Attack now, pagans, we shall conquer them!'
The French cry, 'God, how mourn we this brave man!'
                                                    AOI.

CXX

1580 Count Roland, when he sees Sansun is dead,
You may well know what sorrow he must feel.
He spurs his horse, rides headlong at the pagan,
Grips Durendal, worth more than finest gold,
And aims a blow with all the strength he has
1585 Straight at his golden-ornamented helm.
He slices through his head, hauberk and trunk,
Down through the saddle, richly set with gold
And very deeply through the horse's back.
He slays them both despite all blame or praise.
1590 The pagans say, 'This blow has cost us dear.'
Roland replies, 'I cannot love your like;
For on your side there is but pride and wrong.' AOI.

CXXI

There then appeared a native African,
His name Malquiant, son of King Malcuid,
1595 All his equipment made of solid gold;
He shone most brightly of the pagan host.
He sat upon his horse called Saltperdut;
There never was a beast could outrun him.
He strikes Count Anseïs square on the shield,
1600 Cuts through the red and azure quarterings,
Bursting apart the panels of his hauberk,
Runs through his body iron, wood and all.
Dead is the count; his life is over now.
The French say, 'Woe that you were born for this!'

CXXII

1605 Archbishop Turpin rides across the field;
No such priest ever said a holy mass
Who with his own hand did such acts of courage.
He says to the pagan, 'May God send you ill!
You have killed such a man as grieves my heart.'

1610 He spurs his horse who springs to the attack;
     He strikes a blow at the Toledo shield,
     Laying the pagan dead upon the grass.

CXXIII

     From another side comes riding up Grandonie,
     Capuel's son, from Cappadocia.
1615 He sits astride a horse he calls Mormarie,
     Faster is it than any bird that flies.
     Abandoning his reins, he spurs his horse
     And with great force attacks the count Gerin,
     Breaks the red shield the Frank bears round his neck
1620 And rips the hauberk open with his lance,
     Into his body rams the blue ensign
     Laying the Christian dead on a high rock.
     He then kills Gerin's comrade, Count Gerer,
     And Berenger and Guiun de Saint Antoine.
1625 Then he attacks the powerful Duke Austorie,
     Who holds Valence and fiefs along the Rhone,
     Striking him dead. The pagans then rejoice.
     The French knights say, 'Our men are weakening fast.'

CXXIV

     Count Roland, with his bloody sword in hand,
1630 Has clearly heard the French cry of despair;
     He feels such grief as he can scarce contain.
     He shouts to the pagan, 'May God send you ill!
     You have killed one whom I shall sell you dear.'
     He spurs his horse who runs with all his speed.
1635 Whichever one must pay, the warriors clash.

CXXV

     Grandonie was a brave and worthy man,
     As powerful a vassal as e'er fought;
     Then he encounters Roland in his way.
     He knows the count, though he has never seen him,
1640 By his proud aspect and his noble form,
     And by his grace and bearing overall.
     He cannot keep from taking instant fright;
     He tries to flee, but little it avails.

Count Roland strikes with such prodigious power
1645 He splits his helmet down through the nose piece;
He slices through the nose and mouth and teeth,
Body, and hauberk made of Arab mail,
On through the golden saddle's silver bows
And deep into the horse's very back.
1650 He cuts both down beyond recovery.
The men of Spain cry out their grief and sorrow.
The French say, 'Our protector strikes great blows.'

cxxva

†The battle rages, terrifying, fierce,
The French still fighting with their burnished lances.
1655 There had you seen the sorrow of a nation,
So many men are wounded, bloody, dead.
They lie face upwards, downwards, in great piles.
The Saracens can suffer it no more;
Will they or not, they quit the battlefield,
1660 And by main force the French fly in pursuit. Aoi.

cxxvi

The battle rages hot and fearfully.
The French fight on with vigour, angrily,
Cutting off fists, through ribs, the length of spines,
Through clothes and armour, down to living flesh.
1665 On the green grass the bright red blood flows down.
†.   .   .   .   .
'O land of France, Mahomet curse you now!
Above all people, your sons are most brave!'
No pagan fleeing but who cries 'Marsilie!
1670 Now ride, oh king, for we have need of aid!'

cxxvii

Count Roland speaks then to Count Oliver,
'My lord companion, would you grant me this:
Archbishop Turpin is an able knight;
No better lives on earth and under heaven;
1675 He can attack and strike with lance or spear.'
The count replies, 'Now ride we to his aid!'
Whereat the Franks begin to fight again.

Hard are the blows, the swordfights terrible;
There is great slaughter of the Christians now.
1680 Could one have but seen Roland, Oliver,
Flailing their swords and dealing mighty blows!
Archbishop Turpin fights well with his spear.
Those whom they killed one could well estimate
—And it is written in the charts and briefs—
1685 So says the chronicle, four thousand strong.
The first four battles turned out well for them;
The fifth one proved to be most desperate.
They all were slain, these noble knights of France,
Except for sixty whom God spared a while.
1690 Dearly they'll sell their lives before they die! Aoi.

CXXVIII

When Roland sees the losses of his men,
On this account he turns to Oliver,
'Tell me, my lord, before God, what you think.
Look at these nobles dead upon the ground;
1695 Well may we weep for our sweet, lovely France,
For of so many lords she is bereft.
Ah, king and friend, would only you were here!
Oliver, brother, what shall we do now?
How can we send the news to Charlemagne?'
1700 Says Oliver, 'I know not how to reach him.
Better to die than they recount our shame.' Aoi.

CXXIX

Roland decides, 'Now I shall sound my horn
And Charles will hear it as he climbs the pass;
I promise you, the Franks will all return.'
1705 Says Oliver, 'The shame would be too great.
And ever a reproach to all your family.
This shame would stay with them their whole life long.
When I suggested it, you would not act;
You will not sound it now with my advice.
1710 To blow it now would be no act of courage.
Besides, look how your arms are smeared with blood.'
Roland replies, 'I have struck many blows.' Aoi.

CXXX

Then Roland says, 'This battle is so fierce,
I'll blow the horn; King Charlemagne will hear it.'
1715 Oliver says, 'There's no courage in that.
You did not deign to do it when I asked.
Were the king here, we would not have such losses.
Those who fought with us here are not to blame.'
Then Oliver goes on, 'Now by my beard,
1720 If e'er I see my lovely sister Alde,
You'll never lie between her loving arms!' AOI.

CXXXI

Roland replies, 'Why are you angry with me?'
Oliver answers, 'Comrade, through your fault.
For courage mixed with prudence is not foolish,
1725 And moderation betters recklessness.
French knights are dead through your foolhardiness
And Charles will never have our service more.
Had you believed me, Charles would now be here;
We should have won a victory on this field
1730 And either taken or else killed Marsilie.
Would we had never known your mighty prowess!
Now Charlemagne will have our help no more.
'Til judgement day there'll be no more like him.
You will die here and France will be dishonoured.
1735 With us the loyal company will vanish;
Ere night we'll say a sorrowful adieu.' AOI.

CXXXII

Archbishop Turpin heard their quarrelling
And, setting to his horse the golden spurs,
He rode up to them and rebuked them thus;
1740 'Lord Roland and you too, Lord Oliver,
I beg you, in God's name, don't quarrel here!
To blow the horn at this point serves us little,
But nonetheless it seems the better course.
Let the king come; he can avenge us then;
1745 The men of Spain must not withdraw content.
Our French will come; dismounting in this place,

They'll find us dead, our bodies hacked and cut.
They'll raise us on our biers upon mule-back,
Shed tears for us of sorrow and of pity,
1750 And bury us in churchyards, holy ground.
We'll not be eaten by wolf, pig or dog.'
Roland replies, 'Lord, your advice is sound.' AOI.

CXXXIII

Count Roland lifts the horn up to his mouth,
Then sets his lips and blows it with great force.
1755 The hills are high; the horn's voice loud and long;
They hear it echoing full thirty leagues.
King Charles and his companions hear it sound.
The king declares, 'Our men are in a battle.'
But Ganelon is there to answer him:
1760 'From any other, this would seem untrue.' AOI.

CXXXIV

Count Roland, with much effort, in great anguish,
Sounds the horn once again despite the pain.
The bright red blood comes bursting from his mouth
His temples close to breaking with the strain.
1765 He holds a horn whose range is great indeed;
Charles hears it as he climbs the pass to France;
Duke Naimes has heard it and the French all listen.
Then says the king, 'I hear the horn of Roland!
If not embattled, never would he sound it!'
1770 But Ganelon replies, 'No battle this!
You are so old, your hair so hoary white,
Such words but make you out to be a child!
You know full well enough the pride of Roland;
A miracle God suffers it this long!
1775 Without your order did he not take Noples?
The Saracens inside came running out
And then gave battle to your faithful vassal.
He cleansed the fields of blood with local streams
In order that his deed might not be noticed.
1780 Why, for a hare he'll blow his horn all day!
He's only boasting now before his peers.

No host on earth would seek a fight with him.
Let us ride on. Why do you stop this way?
The land of France is very far ahead.' AOI.

CXXXV

1785 But by now Roland's bleeding at the mouth;
The temples of his brain are broken through;
He sounds his horn with anguish and with pain.
Charles hears it and his French knights listen too.
The king declares, 'This horn sounds loud and long.'
1790 Duke Naimes replies, 'A brave man's in distress.
Now I am sure a battle's being fought;
The treason's his who'd have you hesitate!
So arm yourself and shout your battle-cry!
And ride to help your noble household knights!
1795 For it is Roland that you hear lament!'

CXXXVI

The emperor sounds assembly on his horns;
The French dismount and put their armour on,
Their hauberks, helmets, and their golden swords.
They all bear noble shields and great strong lances
1800 With gonfanons of white and red and blue.
Then all the army's barons mount their horses,
Spur at top speed the whole length of the pass,
While none but tells the man who rides beside,
'If we should see Count Roland ere he dies,
1805 Together with him we shall strike great blows.'
What does it matter? They've delayed too long.

CXXXVII

†The sky that afternoon shines clear and bright.
The armour of the knights reflects the sun,
Their hauberks, helmets, flashing in the light,
1810 Their shields all painted with designs of flowers,
Their lances and their gilded gonfanons.
The emperor rides on in sorrow and wrath,
The French lamenting and their anger stirred.
Not one of them but cries most piteously

1815 And entertains great fear for Roland's life.
The king has Ganelon made prisoner
And hands him over to the household cooks.
He gives his orders to their chief, Besgun:
'Guard him for me just like the knave he is!
1820 It is my household that he has betrayed.'
Besgun takes charge and to the task he sets
A hundred kitchen comrades, best and worst.
The cooks pluck at his beard and his moustache
And each one strikes him four blows with his fist;
1825 They beat him well with cudgels and with sticks,
Then put an iron collar round his neck
And chain him fast just as they would a bear.
In shame they toss him on a sumpter mule.
They'll guard him till they give him back to Charles.

CXXXVIII

1830 High are the hills, immense and shadowy, Aoi.
Deep the ravines, the rivers flowing swift.
The trumpets sound behind them and before
And all give echo to the olifant.
The emperor is riding furiously,
1835 As do the French in sorrow and anger both;
And to a man they weep and show their grief,
Praying to God that Roland should be spared
Until they meet upon the battlefield;
Together what a battle they will fight!
1840 What does it matter? Naught avails them now.
Too long they've stayed; they cannot come in time. Aoi.

CXXXIX

King Charles rides on in fury and distress,
*Upon his cuirass lies his whitening beard.
Eagerly, all the lords of France spur on,
1845 Not one of them but speaks his grief and anger
That they cannot be with their captain Roland
In combat with the Saracens of Spain:
*'If he is hurt, I think none other lives.
Ah God, those sixty nobles in his band!
1850 No king nor captain e'er had better men!' Aoi.

CXL

Roland looks out across the peaks and hills.
He sees so many Frenchmen lying dead,
He mourns them like the noble knight he is:
'May God have mercy on you, barons, lords!
1855 May He grant paradise to all your souls
And let them lie at rest in holy flowers!
Better vassals than you I never saw,
For you have served me faithfully so long
And conquered for King Charles so many lands!
1860 Woe that he fostered you to meet this fate!
Oh land of France, oh blissful, pleasant land,
Today laid desolate by such cruel waste!
*Brave French, I see you die on my account,
And I unable to protect your lives!
1865 May God, the Ever-Faithful, aid you now!
Oliver, brother, you I must not fail,
Or I shall die of grief unless I'm slain.
My lord companion, back now to the fight!'

CXLI

Count Roland has returned now to the field.
1870 With Durendal in hand, he bravely fights.
He cuts Faldrun de Pui straight down the middle
And twenty-four more of the most renowned;
None ever was more eager for revenge.
Just as the deer will fly before the pack,
1875 The pagans flee before the sword of Roland.
Archbishop Turpin says, 'You fight so well,
Such is the valour every knight should have,
Whoe'er bears arms or sits astride a horse.
In battle one must be both strong and fierce,
1880 Or else he is not worth four deniers' weight,
And should be cloistered in a monastery
And daily offer prayers up for our sins.'
Roland replies, 'Attack, and spare no man!'
The French, on hearing this, renew the fight.
1885 There is great slaughter of the Christians now.

CXLII

A man who knows no prisoners will be taken
In such a battle puts up strong defence.
And so the Franks fight on as fierce as lions.
Behold Marsilie in hero's armour now,
1890 Astride the war-horse that he calls Gaignun,
Rides forward, spurring to attack Bevon,
Who was the lord of Belne and of Digun.
His shield he shatters, tears the hauberk through
†And strikes him dead with but this single blow.
1895 Then King Marsilie kills Ivoeries and Count Ives
Together with Girart de Rossillon.
Count Roland, who's not far away from him,
Says to the pagan, 'May God send you ill!
You do great wrong to kill my comrades here;
1900 You'll have a blow for that before we part,
And of my sword today you'll learn the name.'
He then attacks him as a brave man should;
The count strikes off the pagan king's right hand.
He cuts the head off Jurfaleu the Blond
1905 —This pagan was a son of King Marsilie—
The pagans cry, 'Mahomet, save us now!
Oh God, our God, avenge us on King Charles!
Into our land he's sent such wicked villains
Not even death can make them quit the field!'
1910 They say to one another, 'Let us flee!'
Whereat some hundred thousand run away.
Whoever calls them back, they will not come. Aoi.

CXLIII

What does it matter? If Marsilie is fled,
His uncle Marganice has stayed behind,
1915 The lord of Carthage, Alfrere, Garmalie,
And Ethiopia, a cursed land
Whose black-skinned people are beneath his sway;
They have large noses and great outstretched ears;
Together they are more than fifty thousand.
1920 Fiercely, with angry zeal they ride along
And shout aloud the pagan battle cry.

Says Roland, 'Here we'll take our martyrdom,
For now I know we have not long to live.
Accursed who first does not sell dear his life!
1925 Attack, my lords! Strike with your polished swords;
Dispute your deaths and so defend your lives
That by our acts sweet France be not dishonoured!
When my lord Charles will come upon this field,
He'll see such slaughter of the Saracens
1930 —Fifteen of them for every one of us—
He will not fail to bless us every one.' AOI.

CXLIV

When Roland sees that race of infidels
—Each one of them is blacker far than ink,
Their teeth the only feature that shows white—
1935 The count concludes, 'Now do I know in truth
That we shall die today; I know it well.
Attack, oh Franks, and I once more with you!'
Shouts Oliver, 'The devil take the slow.'
At this the French all leap to the attack.

CXLV

1940 But when the pagans see how few the French,
Among them there is haughty confidence.
'The emperor is wrong,' each tells the other.
Then Marganice, upon a sorrel horse,
Urges it on with spurs of purest gold,
1945 And squarely in the back strikes Oliver.
Smashing the shining hauberk through his body,
He rams the lance point straight out through his chest.
The pagan says, 'This time you feel the blow.
Unlucky was the day Charles left you here.
1950 He's done us ill; of that he must not boast.
On you alone have I avenged our dead.'

CXLVI

Oliver knows he has a fatal wound.
He still holds shining Halteclere in his hand;
He strikes the pointed helm of Marganice

1955 —The flowers and gems fly off on every side—
And splits his head in half from top to teeth.
He lifts his sword and strikes the pagan dead,
Then after says, 'Woe to you Saracen!
I do not say Charles has not suffered loss,
1960 But to no wife nor lady you have seen
Within your kingdom will you ever boast
A denier's worth you killed me with one blow
Or injured me or any other man.'
With that he cries aloud for Roland's help. Aoi.

CXLVII

1965 Count Oliver knows that his wound is mortal;
He'll never have his fill of vengeance now.
Amid the press he fights with gallantry.
He cuts through lances and through pagan shields;
He cuts off feet and hands, through saddles, ribs.
1970 Whoever saw him slaughtering Saracens,
Throwing their bodies one atop the other,
Would hold in memory a noble knight.
Not once does he forget Charles' battle-cry;
He shouts 'Montjoie!' in loud and ringing voice.
1975 He calls to Roland as his friend and peer,
'My lord companion, come, ride at my side!
Today in sorrow we'll be separated.' Aoi.

CXLVIII

Count Roland looks upon his comrade's face;
It is discoloured, livid, very pale.
1980 The bright red blood is streaming down his body;
Great clots of blood and flesh fall to the ground.
'God,' says the count, 'I know not what to do.
Alas, your noble courage ends like this!
The man will never live who equals you.
1985 Sweet France, how empty do you stand today
Of noble vassals, how destroyed, cast down!
From this death will the emperor suffer loss.'
He speaks, and faints away across his horse. Aoi.

CXLIX

Behold Count Roland fainted on his horse
1990 And Oliver who bears a mortal wound.
He's bled so much, his sight is clouded, blurred;
Nor near nor far so clear he cannot see
That he might recognize a mortal man.
As Oliver encounters his companion,
1995 He strikes him on his helmet decked in gold
And to the nose guard cuts it in two halves;
The blow's not strong enough to wound his head.
Count Roland, at the blow, looks up at him
And asks him in a gentle, tender voice,
2000 'Lord comrade, did you mean to strike that blow?
For this is Roland, he who ever loved you.
You never spoke a word to challenge me.'
Says Oliver, 'Now I can hear your voice.
I saw you not; may the Lord God see you!
2005 I struck you? Comrade, pardon me the blow!'
Roland replies, 'I felt no pain from it.
Here and before God do I pardon you.'
Upon this word, each bows toward the other.
In such great love behold them separated!

CL

2010 Oliver feels that death is close behind.
Both of his eyes roll upwards in his head,
He loses both his hearing and his sight.
He gets down from his horse, kneels on the ground,
And with great feeling speaks his last confession
2015 Aloud to heaven, both hands joined in prayer:
He asks God that He grant him paradise
And that He bless King Charles and his sweet France
And, over all men, his companion Roland.
His heart fails and his helm sinks on his chest,
2020 His body falls full length upon the ground.
The count is dead; he does not linger more.
The noble Roland weeps, laments for him;
A more grief-stricken man you will not hear.

CLI

Now Roland sees that his great friend is dead,
2025 Lying face down, his face pressed to the ground;
With gentle, tender words he starts to mourn:
'Alas that you were brave, my lord companion!
How many years and days we've been together!
You never did me ill, nor did I you.
2030 Now you are dead; I grieve that I still live.'
Uttering these words, Count Roland faints away
Upon the war horse he calls Veillantif.
His feet are fixed within the golden stirrups;
†However he may lean, he cannot fall.

CLII

2035 Before Roland regains his consciousness
Or can recover fully from his faint,
The losses suffered by the French are clear:
The French are dead; he has lost all of them
Except for Turpin and Gualter del Hum.
2040 Gualter has ridden down from the high mountains
And with the men of Spain fought long and hard.
His men are dead; the pagans overcame them.
He has no choice but to flee down the valleys.
He calls on Roland, asking him for aid:
2045 'Ah, noble count! Where are you, valiant man?
I never was afraid there where you stood.'
Count Gualter calls, who conquered Maëlgut;
'My uncle is the old, white-haired Droün.
I used to be your favourite for my courage.
2050 My lance is broken and my shield is pierced;
My hauberk's torn, its mail is ripped away;
With lance thrusts I am wounded through my body.
I shall die soon, but I've sold my life dear.'
As he says this, Count Roland hears his voice;
2055 *Spurring his horse, he quickly rides to him. AOI.

CLIII

Roland is sorrowful, but in a rage.
Into the press he rides and starts to strike.
Soon he has killed some twenty men of Spain,
And Gualter six and the archbishop five.
2060 The pagans say, 'What wicked, cruel men!
Take care, my lords, they not escape alive!
Accursed whoever fails to attack them now,
A coward he who lets them go scot free!'
The pagans raise the hue and cry once more
2065 And from all sides they ride to the attack. Aoi.

CLIV

Count Roland was a noble warrior,
Gualter del Hum a very valiant knight,
Archbishop Turpin brave, of proven valour;
Not one of them will leave the other two.
2070 Amid the press, they strike the pagans down.
A thousand Saracens dismount to fight
And forty thousand more are mounted still.
I do not think they dare approach the French.
They throw at them their lances and their spears,
2075†A storm of darts and javelins of all sorts.
Gualter del Hum is killed with the first blows.
Turpin de Reins, with all his shield pierced through,
His helmet crushed, is wounded in the head.
His hauberk's torn and stripped of its chain mail;
2080 He's wounded by four spears straight through his
     body.
They kill the war-horse upon which he rides.
There is great anguish when the archbishop falls. Aoi.

CLV

When Turpin knows that he has been struck down,
Wounded straight through the body with four spears,
2085 Quickly the brave man jumps back on his feet.
He looks at Roland and runs back to him,
Saying, 'My lord, I'm not defeated yet,
For no good vassal will give in alive.'

He draws Almace, his sword of burnished steel
2090 And in the battle's heat strikes many blows.
Later Charles said that he did not spare one,
For some four hundred did they find about him,
Some maimed and others stabbed right through the
　　middle,
And many pagans who had lost their heads.
2095 So says the tale, and one who saw the field:
The noble Giles for whom God showed his powers,
Who wrote the charter for the Laon church.
Who knows not that has not well understood.

CLVI

Valiantly Roland carries on the fight,
2100 His body bathed in sweat, his fever high;
Great pain and suffering rack his wounded head,
His temples broken since he blew his horn.
But still he wants to know if Charles will come;
He draws the olifant and feebly blows.
2105 The emperor stands stock still, listening.
'My lords,' says he, 'it goes badly for us.
My nephew will this day be lost to us,
For I hear by the sound he scarcely lives.
Whoever would be with him, ride on swiftly!
2110 Sound all the trumpets that this army has!'
Then sixty thousand of them ring so loud
That mountains echo, valleys give reply.
The pagans hear but do not take it lightly
And each one says, 'Charles will be on us soon.'

CLVII

2115 The pagans say, 'The emperor returns; AOI.
Hark to the trumpets of the men of France.
If Charles returns, then we shall be destroyed;
If Roland lives, we shall have war again.
Now we have lost our lovely land of Spain.'
2120 Four hundred such assemble, wearing helms,
The best of those who wished to keep the field;
They make a strong and fierce attack on Roland;
Now on his side the count has much to do. AOI.

CLVIII

Count Roland, when he sees them coming on,
2125 Turns that much stronger, fiercer, more alert;
He will not yield to them while he still lives.
Astride the horse which men call Veillantif,
He drives him on with spurs of finest gold
And carries his attack into the press,
2130 Along with the archbishop at his side.
Each to the other shouts, 'Ride on now, friend!
We've heard the trumpets of the men of France,
And Charlemagne, the mighty king, returns!'

CLIX

Count Roland never showed a love for cowards,
2135 Nor prideful, nor yet evil, wicked men,
Nor any knight, were he not a good vassal.
He calls out to the archbishop Turpin,
'My lord, you are on foot and I on horse;
For love of you, here will I take my stand.
2140 Together we shall face the good and bad.
I shall not leave your side for mortal man.
Today we'll turn back their assault on them.
The best blows will be those of Durendal.'
Turpin says, 'Woe to him who strikes not well.
2145 King Charles returns; he'll be avenged for us.'

CLX

The pagans cry, 'Alas that we were born!
How fatal has this day now dawned for us!
For we have lost our nobles, lords and peers!
The warrior Charles returns with his great host;
2150 We hear the ringing trumpets of the French;
Loud is the noise as they cry out "Montjoie!"
Count Roland is so warlike and so fierce,
He'll not be overcome by mortal man.
Let's throw our spears at him, then let him be.'
2155 And so they fire a storm of javelins, darts,
A shower of missiles, lances, feathered spears.
They have pierced and destroyed Count Roland's
shield,

Cut through his hauberk, torn the chains of mail,
But still they have not wounded Roland's body.
2160 Veillantif has been struck in twenty places;
They leave him lying dead beneath the count.
The pagans flee; henceforth they'll leave him be;
Count Roland is left standing on his feet. Aoi.

CLXI

The pagans, angry and resentful, flee,
2165 Bending their efforts to their flight toward Spain.
Count Roland has no means to give pursuit,
For he has lost his charger Veillantif.
Will he or not, he is left standing there.
He goes to give his help to the archibishop,
2170 Unlaces and removes his gilded helm
And then takes off the gleaming lightweight hauberk.
†Cutting his tunic off, he tears it up
And with the pieces stops his gaping wounds.
Roland clasps Turpin in a close embrace,
2175 Then lays him carefully down on the grass.
Roland, with greatest gentleness, beseeches,
'Now, noble man, give me your leave to go;
For our companions, whom we loved so much,
Are now all dead; we must not let them lie.
2180 I want to try to go in search of them
And lay them all together here before you.'
Turpin replies, 'You're free to come and go.
The field is yours and mine, thanks be to God.'

CLXII

Count Roland turns, goes through the field alone;
2185 He searches in the valleys, on the peaks,
Finds there Gerin and his comrade Gerer,
Count Berenger and his companion Otes;
He finds Count Anseïs and Duke Sansun
And also old Girart de Rossillon.
2190 He fetches all the barons, one by one,
And each of them he brings to the archbishop;
†There at his feet he lays them out in rows.
Archbishop Turpin cannot help but weep;

He lifts a hand and gives them benediction,
2195 Then says, 'Woe that you were such noble lords!
May God the Glorious One take all your souls,
Put them in paradise mid holy flowers!
As for my death, my great regret is this:
I'll see no more the noble emperor.'

CLXIII

2200 Turning away to search the field again,
Count Roland finds his comrade Oliver.
He clasps him tightly in a close embrace.
As best he can, he takes him to the bishop
And on a shield he lays him by the others.
2205 Archbishop Turpin signs them with the cross.
Then pain and pity grow more grievous still.
Says Roland, 'Noble comrade Oliver,
You were the son of noble Duke Reiner
Who held the frontier called Val de Runers.
2210 In breaking lances and in smashing shields,
In conquering and daunting haughty foes,
In aiding and advising valiant men,
In vanquishing and striking fear in pagans,
In no land is there any better knight.'

CLXIV

2215 Count Roland, when he sees his peers are dead,
And Oliver, whom he had loved so much,
Is seized with pity and begins to weep.
The colour drains completely from his face,
His pain so great, he can no longer stand;
2220 Will he or not, he falls down in a faint.
Says Turpin, 'Woe that you should come to this!'

CLXV

Archbishop Turpin, seeing Roland faint,
Is seized by greater grief than e'er he knew.
He reaches out and takes the olifant.
2225 Through Rencesvals there flows a little stream;
He wants to try to fetch the count some water.
Slowly, with staggering steps, he turns to go;

So feeble is he that he cannot move;
He has no strength; he has lost too much blood.
2230 Before a man could walk but six score feet,
His heart fails; he falls forward on the ground,
While agonizing death envelopes him.

CLXVI

Count Roland reawakens from his faint;
He rises to his feet, but in great pain;
2235 Surveys the hills, looks out across the plain;
On the green grass, beyond his own companions,
He sees the noble barons lying dead,
Among them the archbishop named by God.
Turpin makes his confession, looks on high
2240 Up toward heaven, both hands joined in prayer;
He prays that God will grant him paradise.
Turpin is dead, the warrior of Charles,
In battles and in pious sermons both,
Always a champion against the pagan.
2245 May God grant him His holy benediction! Aoi.

CLXVII

Count Roland sees the archbishop on the ground;
He sees the bowels trailing from his body,
The brains that bubble out upon his forehead.
Upon his bosom, high upon his breast
2250 He crosses Turpin's elegant white hands.
He mourns him deeply in his country's way:
'Ah, noble man, knight of the highest birth,
I now commend you to the Heavenly One.
No man will live who'll freely serve Him more;
2255 Since the apostles, no such man of God
For guarding Holy Truth or winning others.
May suffering and distress not plague your soul;
May heaven's gate be opened wide to it!'

CLXVIII

Now Roland feels his death is very near;
2260 His brains are seeping out through both his ears.
He prays that God call all the peers to Him,

Then he prays to the angel Gabriel.
He takes his horn, that it not be dishonoured,
And in the other hand holds Durendal.
2265 More than the distance of a crossbow shot
He walks across the field, heading toward Spain.
Climbing a hill, he stops beneath a tree;
Four great stone blocks stand there, all cut from
    marble.
On the green grass he falls upon his back
2270 And there he faints, for death is very near.

CLXIX

High are the hills and towering the trees;
Four blocks of marble lying on the ground;
Count Roland lies unconscious on the grass.
But all the while a pagan has been watching,
2275 As, feigning death, he lay among the rest,
His face and body smeared and daubed with blood.
He rises to his feet and runs along,
A pagan grand and strong and very brave,
Who in his pride conceives a mortal anger.
2280 He seizes Roland's body and his arms
And says, 'The nephew of King Charles is conquered.
I'll carry to Arabia this sword.'
But Roland feels him draw the weapon out.

CLXX

Now Roland feels the pagan take his sword.
2285 Opening his eyes, he says but this to him,
'I do not think you can be one of ours.'
Seizing the horn he never hoped to lose,
He strikes the pagan on his golden helm;
Smashing the helmet's steel, his head and bones,
2290 He drives the pagan's eyes out of his head
And knocks him over dead right at his feet.
'Ignoble pagan, how were you so bold
To seize me with no thought of right or wrong?
No man will hear it but will think you mad.
2295 My olifant is split at the wide end,
The crystal and the gold have fallen out.'

CLXXI

Now Roland feels that he has lost his sight.
Summoning all his strength, he gains his feet;
The colour of his face has drained away.
2300 A dark grey rock lies on the ground before him;
He strikes ten blows on it in bitter grief.
The sword's steel grates, but neither breaks nor notches.
'Ah!' cries the count, 'Holy Saint Mary, help me!
Alas, good Durendal, what fate is yours!
2305 For, dying now, I cannot care for you.
With you how many battles have I won!
With you how many wide lands have I conquered!
Lands held by Charles whose beard is hoary white.
May none who flees before another have you!
2310 A faithful vassal held you for so long!
Never will blessed France see such another.'

CLXXII

Count Roland strikes on the sardonyx stone;
Though the steel grates, it neither breaks nor notches.
When Roland sees he cannot break his sword,
2315 Then he begins to mourn it to himself;
'Ah, Durendal, so lovely, shining, bright!
In the sun's rays you gleam and flash with light.
King Charles was in the vale of Moriane
When God sent word from heaven by His angel
2320 That he should give you to a captain count.
The noble, mighty king bound you on me.
With you I conquered Anjou, Brittany,
With you I conquered Poitou and then Maine,
With you I conquered noble Normandy,
2325 With you I conquered Provence, Aquitaine,
All Lombardy, the province of Romagna;
With you I conquered Flanders and Bavaria,
And Burgundy and all Apulia,
Constantinople which to Charles does homage
2330 And Saxony where all he asks is done;
With you I conquered Scotland, Ireland too,
And England which he holds as his own land.

With you I've conquered many lands and countries
Which Charles now holds whose beard is snowy white.
2335 For this my sword I feel great grief and woe.
I'd sooner die than it belong to pagans.
Oh God, let France not be disgraced by that!'

CLXXIII

Roland strikes once again on the dark stone,
Knocking more pieces off than I could tell.
2340 The steel grates but it neither breaks nor shatters;
Each time the sword rebounds into the air.
When the count sees that he will never break it,
Then to himself most gently he laments:
'Ah, Durendal, how beautiful, how holy!
2345 Such relics are there in your golden hilt:
Saint Peter's tooth, holy Saint Basil's blood,
Hair from the head of my lord Saint Denis,
A piece of clothing from the Blessed Virgin.
It is not right that infidels should wield you;
2350 You should be served by Christian men alone.
May none have you who might be cowardly!
For I have conquered many lands with you
Which Charles now holds whose beard is white with
   age;
Through them the emperor is noble, strong.'

CLXXIV

2355 Count Roland feels death overcoming him;
It moves down from his head toward his heart.
†As quickly as he can, beneath the pine
He lies down on his face in the green grass.
He puts his sword and horn beneath his body
2360 And turns his head toward the pagan host.
This he does for he wishes earnestly
That Charles, arriving with his host, should say
He died a conqueror, this noble count.
At frequent intervals he makes confession
2365 And for his sins he offers God his glove. Aoi.

CLXXV

Now Roland feels his time is nearly gone;
On a steep hill he lies, his face toward Spain;
And with one hand he strikes upon his breast:
†'God, I have sinned against thy holy laws
2370 Through all my sins, the greater and the less,
Which since my hour of birth I have committed
Until this day when I am here struck down.'
He holds his right glove out toward his God;
Angels descend from heaven to his side. Aoi.

CLXXVI

2375 Roland the count lies underneath a pine.
His face is turned toward the land of Spain.
His mind begins to call up many things:
The lands he conquered as a warrior,
Sweet France his land, his family and line,
2380 And Charlemagne, his lord, who brought him up.
He cannot help but weep and heave great sighs.
But he does not forget his own soul's health;
He makes confession, asking for God's grace:
'True Father, who did ever keep the faith,
2385 Who raised Saint Lazarus from out the grave,
Who rescued Daniel from the lion's mouth,
Protect my soul from every peril raised
By all the sins that in my life I did.'
He offers up his right glove unto God;
2390 Saint Gabriel comes to take it from his hand.
Now Roland lays his head down on his arm;
With his hands joined, he goes to meet his end.
God sends below his angel Cherubin
With Saint Michel du Péril de la Mer;
2395 The archangel Saint Gabriel comes with them;
They bear the count's soul up to paradise.

CLXXVII

Roland is dead. God has his soul in heaven.
The emperor Charles arrives at Rencesvals.
There is no road nor by-way in the place,

2400 No empty field, nor ell, nor foot of ground
That is not heaped with bodies, French or pagan.
Charles cries aloud, 'Where are you, dearest nephew?
Where the archbishop and Count Oliver?
Where is Gerin and Gerer his companion?
2405 And where is Otes and the Count Berenger?
Ives and Ivoeries whom I have held so dear?
What has become of Gascon Engeler,
Duke Sansun and the noble Anseïs?
Where is my old Girart de Rosillon?
2410 Where are the twelve peers whom I had left behind?'
What use his cries, when no one answers him?
Says Charles, 'Now have I cause to be disheartened
That I was not here at the battle's start.'
†He tears his beard like one beset with grief.
2415 So many noble knights let fall great tears,
And twenty thousand, fainting, fall to earth.
Duke Naimes feels boundless pity for them all.

CLXXVIII

Among them there is neither knight nor noble
Who does not weep most bitterly from grief;
2420 They weep for sons, for brothers and for nephews,
And for their friends and for their own liege lords;
Many of them fall fainting to the ground.
Duke Naimes acts nobly upon seeing this,
And first of all says to the emperor:
2425 'Look there ahead, my lord, two leagues from us.
You can see from the great roads billowing dust
That many of the pagan host are gone.
Now ride, my lord, avenge this grief and woe!'
'Oh God,' says Charles, 'since they are so far off,
2430 Grant me this chance for honour and for right;
The flower of sweet France have they taken from me.'
The king gave orders to Gebuin, Otun,
Tedbald de Reins and to the count Milun:
'Mount guard upon this field, both vales and hills.
2435 Let all our dead lie there just as they are.
See that no lion nor wild beast disturbs them,
Nor squire nor servant lay a hand on them;

And I forbid that any man should touch them
Until God will that we regain this field.'
2440 They answer gently in their love for Charles:
'True emperor, dear lord, we'll do your will.'
A thousand knights they hold back for this duty. Aoi.

CLXXIX

The emperor now has his trumpets sound,
Then the brave man rides out with his great host.
2445 †Some of the men of Spain have turned their back;
The French, acting as one, press the pursuit.
When the king sees the night about to fall,
He dismounts on the green grass of a field
And, kneeling there, he prays to the Lord God
2450 To make the sun stop in its course for him,
Hold off the night and make the daylight last.
Behold an angel who oft spoke with Charles
†Quickly appeared and gave him this command:
'Ride on, Charles, for you will not lack for light.
2455 God knows that you have lost the flower of France.
You'll be avenged upon the infidel.'
On hearing this, the emperor remounts. Aoi.

CLXXX

God did great miracles for Charlemagne,
For on that day the sun stayed where it was.
2460 The pagans flee, the French hot in pursuit.
They overtake them at Val Tenebrus
And, striking blows, chase them to Saragoce.
With powerful blows they kill them as they ride,
Cut off their side paths and the larger roads.
2465 Suddenly, Ebro's waters loom ahead,
Frightful and deep and flowing very fast.
There is no barge nor ship of any sort.
The pagans call on their god Tervagant
†And plunge straight in; but hopeless is their case.
2470 Some armoured men, the heaviest of all,
Sink to the bottom of the river bed;
The other pagans float away downstream.

Those who fare best still drink more than their fill
And all are drowned in frightful suffering.
2475 The French cry out, 'Alas, unhappy Roland!' Aoi.

CLXXXI

When Charles sees that the pagans all are dead,
Large numbers killed and many of them drowned,
And that great booty falls now to his knights,
The noble king, dismounting from his horse,
2480 Kneels on the ground and offers thanks to God.
When he lifts up his head, the sun has set.
The king says, 'Let us make camp here tonight;
It is too late now to reach Rencesvals.
Tired are our horses, worn out and exhausted;
2485 Take off their saddles and their halters too
And let them graze at will amid these fields.'
The French reply, 'My lord, your words are sound.'
                                                    Aoi.

CLXXXII

The emperor has set up his encampment;
The French descend into the empty fields.
2490 They have removed the saddles from their mounts,
Taken the golden halters from their heads.
They turn them loose amid fresh meadow grass;
Tonight they cannot give them further care.
Whoever's tired sleeps stretched out on the ground.
2495 They mount no watch around the camp this night.

CLXXXIII

The emperor has lain down in a field;
He places his great lance close by his head;
The noble man will not disarm tonight;
He still is dressed in damascened hauberk,
2500 Still laced his golden-ornamented helm,
Joiuse still belted on, the peerless sword
Which daily changes colour thirty times.
Long could we speak and tell about that lance
With which Our Lord was wounded on the cross;
2505 Charles has its metal point, by God's own grace,
Set in the golden pommel of his sword;

For this distinction and for its great worth,
The name ' Joiuse' was given to this blade.
Of this the Frankish lords are ever mindful;
2510 From it they have their battle cry 'Montjoie!'
No foemen for that reason can resist them.

CLXXXIV

The night is clear and brightly shines the moon.
Charles has lain down, but still he grieves for Roland,
And Oliver weighs heavy on his heart
2515 With the twelve peers and all those men of France
Whom, bloody, dead, he left at Rencesvals.
He cannot help but weep and mourn for them.
He prays to God that He preserve their souls.
Weary the king, his suffering is great;
2520 He falls asleep, too tired to take a step.
O'er all the fields now Frankish barons sleep.
No horse is there who can stand on his feet;
Those that want grass, chew on it lying down.
He has learned much who knows the pain of struggle.

CLXXXV

2525 King Charles is sleeping like a man exhausted.
But God has sent Saint Gabriel to his side,
Commanding him to guard the emperor.
The angel spends the whole night by his head
And through a vision he reveals to Charles
2530 A battle that against him will be fought.
In painful terms he shows the battle's meaning.
Charles, in his dream, looks up toward the sky;
He hears the thunder, feels the winds and frosts;
He sees both violent storms and frightful tempests,
2535 While fire and flames appear before his eyes
And, burning, quickly fall upon his host.
The ash and fruitwood lances start to burn
With all the shields down to the golden boss;
The shafts of the sharp lances crumble away,
2540 While hauberks and steel helmets twist, contort.
Charles sees his knights in anguish and great pain.
Then bears and leopards come to eat them up,

Along with snakes and vipers, dragons, devils;
Griffons there are, some thirty thousand strong,
2545 Not one of them but swoops down on the French.
The knights cry out to Charlemagne for help;
The king is filled with grief and pity for them.
He tries to go to help, but he is stopped;
Down from a hill a lion charges him
2550 —A beast most terrible and proud and fierce—
He seeks out and attacks the king himself.
They seize each other, both arms locked in struggle.
He cannot know which one will win, which fall;
The emperor sleeps on and does not wake.

CLXXXVI

2555 Thereafter comes to him a second vision:
He stands upon the palace steps at Aix,
Holding a bear cub fastened by two chains.
Down from Ardennes he sees come thirty bears,
Each one of them is speaking like a man.
2560 They say to him, 'Lord, give him back to us.
It is not right that he should stay with you;
We must be prompt to help one of our own.'
From out the palace runs a hunting dog,
Assaults the very largest of the bears
2565†On the green grass, charging through his companions.
Then the king sees a frightful battle rage.
He does not know which one will win, which lose.
God's angel now has shown the king his vision.
Charles sleeps until the dawning of the morrow.

CLXXXVII

2570 The king Marsilie has fled to Saragoce.
Dismounting underneath an olive's shade,
He takes off sword, helmet and tunic too,
And lies down on the grass most miserably.
He has completely lost his whole right hand;
2575 He feels great pain and faints from loss of blood.
Before him is his wife, Queen Bramimonde
Who weeps and cries and sorely grieves for him.
The more than twenty thousand men with her

Call curses down on Charles and on sweet France.
2580 They run to Apollo in his vaulted chamber;
They rail at him, insult him terribly:
'Ah, evil god, why cause us such great shame?
Why do you let our king be so defeated?
You give a poor reward to who serves best.'
2585 They take Apollo's sceptre and his crown.
At once they hoist him up atop a column,
Then topple him to earth among their feet,
And with great clubs they smash him into pieces.
They tear the carbuncle from Tervagant
2590 And push Mahomet down into a ditch
Where dogs and pigs may bite and trample him.

CLXXXVIII

King Marsilie has recovered from his faint.
He has himself borne to his vaulted chamber,
A room in many colours decorated.
2595 Queen Bramimonde laments and weeps for him;
She tears her hair, bewails her woeful state
And thereupon she cries with a loud voice:
'Ah, Saragoce, today you are deprived
Of the most noble king who governed you!
2600 Our very own gods have done you great ill,
Who on this morning failed him in the battle.
The emir Baligant will be a coward
If he does not fight with this daring host
Who are so proud they care not for their lives.
2605 The emperor, he of the long white beard,
Is very brave and shows great recklessness;
If there is battle, he will never flee.
Alas that there lives no man who can kill him!'

CLXXXIX

The emperor, through his prodigious power,
2610 Has been in Spain for fully seven years
Where he has taken castles, many towns.
King Marsilie took a necessary step:
In the first year he sent his letters sealed
To Babylon, calling on Baligant—

2615 The old emir of great antiquity
  *Who had outlived Homer and Virgil both—
  To come and succour him at Saragoce;
  Would Baligant not come, he'd leave his gods
  And all the idols that he had adored
2620 And would receive the Christian law and faith
  And reconcile himself with Charlemagne.
  But, far away, the emir tarried long,
  Sent for his host in forty different lands,
  Ordered his mighty galleys be prepared,
2625†With barges and with warships of all kinds.
  In the seaport at Alexandria,
  He has his fleet assembled and prepared,
  And then, in May, on the first day of summer,
  He launches forth his host upon the sea.

CXC

2630 Great are the armies of this heathen race;
  They sail and row and steer with strength and vigour.
  Atop the masts and from the lofty prows
  *Carbuncles shine amid the glow of lanterns;
  They throw aloft a blaze that shines so bright,
2635 The sea's more beautiful by night than day;
  When the fleet comes upon the Spanish coast,
  The countryside reflects the light, grows bright.
  News of the landing reaches King Marsilie. Aoi.

CXCI

  The pagan force does not delay nor wait;
2640 They leave the sea, embark upon fresh water;
  Leaving behind both Marbrise and Marbrose,
  They turn their ships upstream along the Ebro.
  There are so many lanterns and carbuncles,
  All the night long they give the ships much light.
2645 They anchor the same day at Saragoce. Aoi.

CXCII

  The day is radiant and the sun shines bright.
  The emir Baligant steps from his lighter,
  The lord Espaneliz at his right hand;

Seventeen kings follow along his way
2650 With I know not how many counts and dukes.
Beneath a laurel set amid a field,
They throw a white silk robe on the green grass
And on it place an ivory faldstool.
Thereupon sits the pagan Baligant
2655 And all the others standing round about.
Their suzerain is first to speak aloud:
'Now listen to me, noble, worthy knights!
King Charles, the emperor of all the Franks,
Should not eat if I do not give him leave.
2660 Throughout Spain he has waged fierce war on me.
Now I intend to seek him out in France;
I shall not stop nor stay while yet I live,
Till he be dead or, living still, give up.'
Upon his knee he strikes with his right glove.

CXCIII

2665 After he spoke, he stubbornly resolved
That he would not desist for all earth's gold
Until he went to Aix where Charles held court;
His men advise and counsel him in this.
Then he calls forward two of his own knights,
2670 One Clarifan, the other Clarïen:
'You are the sons of the king Maltraien
Who willingly was my ambassador.
I order you to go to Saragoce
And say this to Marsilie on my behalf:
2675 I have come to his aid against the French;
If I find the occasion, battle follows.
And give this folded golden glove to him;
Put it upon Marsilie's own right hand;
Bear him this staff made of the purest gold,
2680 Then let him come to renew his allegiance.
I go now into France to battle Charles.
If by my grace he kneels not at my feet
And still abandons not the Christian faith,
Then I shall take the crown from off his head.'
2685 The pagans answer, 'Sire, your words are good.'

CXCIV

Says Baligant, 'And now to horse, my lords!
One bear the glove, the other one the staff!'
They answer him, 'My lord, we'll do your will.'
The pagan envoys ride to Saragoce,
2690 Passing ten gates, four bridges on their way,
Riding through streets where bourgeois live and work.
As they ride up toward the stronghold's walls,
They hear a murmuring from within the palace.
Uncounted numbers of the pagan folk
2695 Are weeping, shouting, showing their great grief,
Railing against Mahomet, Tervagant,
†Apollo, gods who have abandoned them.
Each of the other asks, 'What now, oh wretch?
For utter ruin now has come upon us,
2700 And we have lost our noble king Marsilie;
Yesterday Roland cut his right hand off;
And Jurfaleu the Blond is lost to us.
Today the Franks have all Spain in their power.'
The messengers dismount upon the step.

CXCV

2705 They leave their mounts beneath an olive tree;
Two Saracens come forth to take the reins.
Each messenger then holds the other's cloak;
And they walk up into the lofty palace.
Just as they go into the vaulted room,
2710 They give the king, in good faith, ill-timed greetings:
'May Mahomet, who holds us in his power,
And Tervagant and lord Apollo too
Now save the king and keep watch o'er the queen.'
Says Bramimonde, 'What foolishness I hear!
2715 These our own gods have given up our cause.
At Rencesvals they showed poor miracles
And let our knights all perish in that place;
They failed my own lord on the battlefield.
He lost his right hand, all of his right hand!
2720 It was the powerful Roland cut it off.

Now Charles will have all Spain within his power.
What will become of this unhappy woman?
Would that there were a man to kill Charles for me!'
AOI.

CXCVI

Says Clarïen, 'My lady, speak not so!
2725 We are ambassadors from Baligant;
He sends word that he will protect Marsilie
And, as a sign, sends this his glove and staff.
We have four thousand ships upon the Ebro,
Swift galleys, warships, barges of all sorts,
2730 And dromunds more than I could tell the number.
The emir is all-powerful and mighty;
He will invade France, seeking Charlemagne.
He plans to kill him or to make him yield.'
Says Bramimonde, 'No need to travel far!
2735 You'll find the French much closer to this place.
They've been here in this land full seven years!
The emperor's a brave and warlike lord;
He'd sooner die than flee the battlefield.
No king 'neath heaven but whom he counts a child;
2740 Charles fears no man alive upon the earth.'

CXCVII

'Enough of this!' cries out the king Marsilie.
He says, 'Ambassadors, now speak to me!
†You see my anguish and my wounds are mortal;
Nor is there left to me son, daughter, heir.
2745 I had a son, and he was killed last night.
Say to my lord that he come here to see me.
The emir has rights over all of Spain;
My rights do I renounce, if he will take her.
But then he must defend her from the Franks!
2750 I'll give him good advice about King Charles;
Within a month you will have conquered him.
You'll bear the city keys to Baligant.
Then say, if he believes me, he'll not leave.'
The messengers reply, 'You speak the truth.' AOI.

CXCVIII

2755 Then says Marsilie, 'The emperor of France
Has slain my men and laid waste to my land,
Broken my cities' walls and ravaged them.
Last night he lay close by the Ebro's stream,
Not more, I know, than seven leagues away.
2760 Tell the emir to lead his army there;
Through you I say, let battle there be joined!'
He gives to them the keys of Saragoce;
Then both ambassadors bow low their heads,
And, taking leave, depart upon this word.

CXCIX

2765 The ambassadors have mounted on their horses;
Swiftly they ride outside the city walls
And come in great alarm to the emir.
They hand to him the keys of Saragoce.
Baligant asks, 'What have you found within?
2770 Where is the king Marsilie for whom I sent?'
Says Clarïen, 'He's wounded unto death.
Yesterday Charles was marching through the pass,
Intending to continue into France.
A noble party held the rear for him:
2775 His nephew Roland was left in command;
Count Oliver and the twelve peers were there
With twenty thousand of the knights of France.
The noble king Marsilie gave battle to them;
He was alone with Roland on the field;
2780 With Durendal, Roland gave him a blow
Such that it struck his right hand from his body.
Count Roland killed the son Marsilie so loved
And all the barons that he had led out.
They left in flight, Marsilie could stay no more.
2785 The emperor pursued him long and hard.
The king requests that you come to his aid.
He will renounce to you the Spanish realm.'
The emir Baligant begins to ponder;
So great his grief, he almost is demented. Aoi.

CC

2790 Then Clarïen speaks to him, 'Lord emir,
It was a battle there at Rencesvals.
Roland is dead and the count Oliver
And all the twelve peers whom Charles held so dear.
Some twenty thousand of the French are dead.
2795 King Marsilie lost his right hand in the fight;
The emperor pursued him long and hard;
In this land there is not a single knight
Who was not killed or drowned in Ebro's flood.
The French are now encamped upon the bank.
2800 They are so near us in this very place,
If you will, they'll return home in great grief.'
Baligant's look grows fierce on hearing this,
Though joyous and delighted is his heart.
He rises from the faldstool to his feet
2805 And shouts aloud, 'My lords, tarry no more!
Out of the ships! Mount up, my lords! To horse!
If now old Charlemagne does not take flight,
The king Marsilie will be avenged this day.
For his right hand, I'll give him Charles' own head!'

CCI

2810 The Arab pagans issue from their ships
And, mounted on their horses and their mules,
They ride away, for duty calls them on.
Then Baligant, who set them on their way,
Calls Gemalfin, a favourite knight of his:
2815 'I charge you with assembling the host.'
The emir mounts upon his dark war horse;
He takes along with him four of his dukes
And rides until he reaches Saragoce.
Dismounting there upon a marble block,
2820 While four counts of the city hold his stirrup,
He mounts the front steps of King Marsilie's palace.
Queen Bramimonde comes running out to him,
Cries, 'Would I had not lived to see such grief!
See in what shame, oh sire, I've lost my lord!'
2825 And falls down at his feet. He takes her up
And grieving they go up into the chamber. Aoi.

CCII

The king Marsilie, when he sees Baligant,
Then calls two Spanish Saracens to him:
'Take both my arms and help me to sit up!'
2830 In his left hand he takes one of his gloves.
Then speaks Marsilie, 'My lord, king and emir,
I give back all of Spain into your hands,
With Saragoce, its fiefs and privilege.
I am destroyed and all my host as well.'
2835 The emir replies, 'My sorrow is so great,
I cannot long endure to speak with you.
*I know that Charles expects no war with me,
But nonetheless, I shall accept your glove.'
His grief is such, he turns away and weeps. Aoi.

CCIII

2840 Baligant then descends the palace steps,
Mounts his war horse and spurs toward his host.
He rides until he reaches the front rank;
From time to time he shouts out as he rides,
'Come, pagans, for the French already flee!' Aoi.

CCIV

2845 At morn, when first appears the dawn of day,
Awakes the noble emperor Charlemagne.
Saint Gabriel, whom God has sent to watch him,
Raises a hand and signs him with the cross.
†The king unstraps and lays aside his arms;
2850 Throughout the army, others do the same.
Then they mount up and vigorously ride
Through the long paths, along the wide highroads,
And go to see the awe-inspiring carnage
Upon the battlefield at Rencesvals. Aoi.

CCV

2855 King Charles has now returned to Rencesvals:
He starts to weep for all the dead he finds.
He says then to the French, 'My lords, go slowly,
For I myself must ride ahead alone
Because I dearly wish to find my nephew.

2860 At Aix there was a high feast celebrated
And all my valiant knights made boasts that day
About their battles and their mighty struggles;
And of this matter I heard Roland say
 *That he would never die on foreign soil
2865 Nor yet would he outlive his men and peers;
He'd have his head turned facing his foes' land;
Thus would the baron die a conqueror.'
Farther than one could throw a stick ahead,
Charles rides before the others up a hill.

CCVI

2870 When Charles rode out to seek his nephew Roland,
He found the flowers of many meadow plants
All reddened with the life blood of our barons.
Stricken with pity, he can only weep.
Charles rides up to a point between two trees,
2875 Sees on three rocks the marks of Roland's blows
And, lying on the grass, Roland himself.
No wonder that Charles fills with rage and anguish.
The king dismounts, runs to where Roland lies,
Holding the baron's body with both hands,
2880 Charles faints across him, so intense his grief.

CCVII

The emperor recovers from his faint.
Duke Naimes and Acelin the noble count,
Godefroy d'Anjou and Count Tierri his brother
Take hold of Charles and raise him 'neath a pine.
2885 Charles looks down, sees his nephew lying there,
Then, very gently, fondly, starts to mourn:
'Roland, my friend, God grant his grace to you!
Never has any man seen such a knight
For joining battles and for ending them.
2890 Now is my own fame gone into decline.'
Charles faints again; he cannot help himself. Aoi.

CCVIII

King Charles recovers from his faint once more;
Four of his barons hold him by the hands.

He looks down, sees his nephew lying there,
2895 His noble body, all its colour drained,
His eyes turned up, all dark and full of shadow.
Then Charles laments him with all faith and love:
'Roland, my friend, God place your soul in flowers
Among the glorious in paradise!
2900 What a poor lord you followed into Spain!
The day will never dawn I shall not mourn.
Now how my ardour and my strength will fail!
I shall have no one to sustain my honour.
I do not think I have a single friend;
2905 I have relations, but none is so brave.'
He tears full locks of hair out with both hands.
One hundred thousand Franks are crushed with grief
Such that not one but weeps most bitterly. Aoi.

CCIX

'Roland, my friend, I shall return to France.
2910 When I shall be at Laon at my home,
Then men will come from various foreign parts
And ask, "Where is Roland, the captain count?"
I shall tell them that he has died in Spain.
With difficulty then I'll rule my land;
2915 No day will dawn when I'll not weep and mourn.'

CCX

'Roland, my friend, brave knight and flower of youth,
When I shall be at Aix within my chapel,
Then men will come and ask me news of you.
I'll tell a tale, dreadful and terrible:
2920 My nephew's dead who won my lands for me.
The Saxons will rebel against me then,
Hungarians, Bulgars, all the heathen race,
Men of Palermo, Romans and Apulians,
*Armies of Africa and Califerne;
2925 Then will begin my hardship, toil and woe;
For who will lead my hosts against such might,
When he is dead who always took the fore?
Alas, dear France, how desolate, bereft!

My grief is such, I have no will to live.'
2930 Then he begins to tear at his white beard
And with both hands the hair from his own head.
A hundred thousand French fall fainting down.

CCXI

'On you, Roland, my friend, may God have mercy,
And may your soul be put in paradise!
2935 He who killed you brought ruin to our France.
My grief is such, I have no wish to live.
My noble household, slaughtered all for me!
May God but grant, the Son of Holy Mary,
That, e'er I come upon the Col de Size,
2940 This day my soul be parted from my body
And it be placed among my cherished dead
So that my flesh be buried next to theirs!'
Charlemagne, weeping, tears at his white beard.
Duke Naimes declares, 'His grief is deeply felt.' Aoi.

CCXII

2945 Godefroy d'Anjou says, 'Lord and emperor
Do not display your grief so piteously.
Throughout the field have all our men sought out
Whom Saracens have slaughtered in the battle,
And have them borne into a charnel house.'
2950 The king agrees, 'Now sound your horn, my lord.'
Aoi.

CCXIII

Godefroy d'Anjou then blows a trumpet blast;
The French assemble and Charles gives commands;
They find all of their friends whom pagans slew
And bear them forthwith to a charnel house,
2955 —Many among them bishops, abbots too,
—Both monks and canons, tonsured priests as well—
Pray for their souls and bless them in God's name.
They offer myrrh and light incense for them,
Vigorously incense them one and all,
2960 And then with highest honours bury them.
Thus did they leave them. What else could they do?
Aoi.

CCXIV

The emperor lays Roland side by side
With Oliver and Archbishop Turpin.
Before his eyes he has their bodies opened,
2965 Their hearts removed and wrapped in silken cloths,
And all laid in a coffin of white marble.
The French then take the barons' bodies up
And wrap the noble lords in hides of deer,
Washing the bodies thoroughly with wine.
2970 The king gives orders to Tedbald, Gebuin,
To Count Milun and to the marquis Otes:
'In three carts draw them with us on our way.'
†They all are covered with a precious silk. Aoi.

CCXV

When Charles is ready to set out for France,
2975 The pagan vanguard suddenly appears.
Among the first, there come two messengers
Who tell him that the emir will do battle:
'Oh haughty king, you cannot leave this field!
See now how Baligant rides after you!
2980 Great are the hosts he brings from Araby.
We'll test your courage ere the day is out!' Aoi.

CCXVI

King Charles, running his fingers through his beard,
Thinks and recalls the grief and slaughter here.
Proudly he looks about at all his knights,
2985 Then cries out loudly in a ringing voice:
'My lords of France, to horses and to arms!' Aoi.

CCXVII

The emperor is first to don his arms.
Quickly he dresses in his coat of mail,
Laces his helmet and girds on Joiuse
2990 Which never hides its light despite the sun,
Hangs his Viterbo shield around his neck,
Seizes his lance, brandishes high its shaft,
And mounts upon his war horse Tencendur.

—Charles won him at the fords below Marsune
2995 Where he struck dead Malpalin of Narbonne—
He drops the reins, spurs his horse eagerly,
†Springs forward, his whole army looking on; Aoi.
He calls on God and the apostle of Rome.

CCXVIII

Throughout the field the men of France dismount;
3000 More than one hundred thousand arm together.
They have equipment suiting need and station:
Swift horses and the finest knightly arms.
†Confident in their skill in war, they mount;
For, should they find the chance, they mean to fight.
3005 The gonfanons hang down over their helms.
When King Charles sees these handsome, noble faces,
Then he remarks to Jozeran de Provence,
And to Duke Naimes and Antelme de Maience:
'A man must trust in vassals such as these;
3010 Only a fool would feel despair with them.
Unless the Saracens have second thoughts,
We shall repay them well for Roland's death.'
Duke Naimes replies, 'May God grant that to us!'
                                                   Aoi.

CCXIX

Charles calls upon Rabel and Guineman,
3015 And says to them, 'My lords, I order you
To take the posts of Oliver and Roland.
One bear the sword, the other one the horn,
And ride before us in the foremost rank.
With you there will be fifteen thousand French,
3020 Young men among our bravest and our best.
After these there'll be just as many more
And Gebuin and Lorain will lead them on.'
Thereupon Naimes and the count Jozeran
Busy themselves with forming the divisions.
3025 If they find the occasion, they'll fight hard. Aoi.

CCXX

The first divisions are formed by the French.
After these two they set up yet a third;

In it are vassals from Bavaria;
They estimate its strength at twenty thousand.
3030 In their positions fighting will not slacken;
There is no people that Charles holds more dear
Except the men of France who won these kingdoms.
Oger the Dane, a mighty warrior,
Commands them, for this company is proud. Aoi.

CCXXI

3025 Now three divisions has the emperor Charles.
Then the duke Naimes establishes a fourth
Made up of lords who have distinguished courage:
In it there are the knights of Germany.
The others set their strength at twenty thousand,
3040 All well supplied with horses and with arms.
They will not flee the fight for fear of death.
Herman the Duke of Trace is their commander;
This man will die before he fails in courage. Aoi.

CCXXII

Duke Naimes and Count Jozeran de Provence.
3045 Set up the fifth division of Norman knights.
They number twenty thousand, say the Franks.
Their arms are beautiful, their horses swift.
These men will never yield for fear of death,
No nation under heaven so strong in battle.
3050 Richard the Old will lead them in the field
And he will strike hard with his sharpened lance. Aoi.

CCXXIII

They form the sixth division all of Bretons;
Some thirty thousand knights they have with them.
The Bretons ride along like noble lords,
3055 Their painted lances topped with gonfanons.
The liege lord of these knights is named Oedun;
He gives his orders to Count Nevelon,
Tedbald de Reins and to the marquis Otes:
'Lead on my host; I give you the command.' Aoi.

CCXXIV

3060 The emperor has six divisions formed;
Now the duke Naimes establishes the seventh
Of Poitevins and barons of Auvergne;
Their strength amounts to forty thousand knights.
They have good horses and the best of arms.
3065 They're in a valley, by a hill, alone;
Charles raises his right hand and blesses them.
Jozeran and Godselme are in command. Aoi.

CCXXV

Naimes has set up the eighth division now,
Composed of Flemings and of Frisian lords;
3070 They number more than forty thousand knights.
In their position, fighting will not cease.
Then says the king, 'These knights will do my service.
Both Rembalt and Lord Hamon de Galice
Will lead them on the field in knightly fashion.' Aoi.

CCXXVI

3075 Now Naimes the duke and the count Jozeran
Have formed the ninth division of brave knights,
Men of Lorraine and men of Burgundy.
They number fifty thousand knights by count.
Their helmets laced, dressed in their coats of mail,
3080 They carry lances short of shaft and strong;
And if the pagans do not hesitate,
These men will fight them, if they offer battle.
Tierri the Duke of Argonne leads them on. Aoi.

CCXXVII

The tenth division is the lords of France,
3085 One hundred thousand of our leading knights,
All strong of body, proud of countenance,
Their heads are hoary and their beards are white;
Dressed in their hauberks, double coats of mail,
Girded with swords of French or Spanish make,
3090 Bearing bright emblems on the finest shields.
They all mount up and cry aloud for battle;
They shout 'Montjoie!' With them is Charlemagne.

*Godefroy d'Anjou now bears the oriflamme;
It was Saint Peter's and was called 'Romaine';
3095 But there it took the new name of 'Montjoie'. AOI.

CCXXVIII

The emperor dismounts from his war horse,
Prostrates himself in the green meadow grass;
He lifts his face toward the rising sun
And calls aloud on God most fervently:
3100 'True Father, now defend me on this day,
You who brought Jonas truly unto safety
From out the whale that had him in its belly,
And who did spare the King of Nineveh
And Daniel also from his awful pain,
3105 When he was shut inside the lions' den,
And the three children from the burning fire.
May Your love on this day be at my side.
If it please You, then in Your mercy grant
I may have vengeance for my nephew Roland.'

CCXXIX

3110 When he has prayed, he rises to his feet
And signs the potent blessing on his head.
The king then mounts upon his swift war horse,
While Jozeran and Duke Naimes hold his stirrup;
Then he takes up his shield and sharpened lance.
3115 Handsome his body, robust and comely both,
His face, noble of mien, is clear and bright.
He rides along with firmest resolution.
The trumpets sound their blast before, behind;
Over them all resounds the olifant.
3120 The French weep in compassion for Count Roland.

CCXXX

The emperor rides nobly, bravely on.
He shows his beard outside his leather tunic;
For love of him, the others do the same;
A hundred thousand French all bear this sign.
3125 They pass among the hills and towering rocks,
By chasms and through ominous defiles.

They issue from the passes, cross the wasteland
To enter the frontiers of Spain itself.
Upon a level plain they take their stand.
3130 The pagan van rides back to Baligant;
A Syrian, his messenger, reports:
'We have seen Charles, the haughty king, my lord;
His men are proud and will not fail him now.
Arm yourself well, for we shall soon have battle!'
3135 †Says Baligant, 'You tell me of great courage.
Now sound the trumpets, that my troops may know.'

CCXXXI

They have the drums beat loud throughout the army,
Bugles and trumpets sounding bright and clear.
The pagans all dismount to arm themselves.
3140 The emir Baligant will not delay;
He dresses in a damascened hauberk,
Laces his helmet, all bedecked with gold,
Lastly he girds a sword at his left side;
To serve his pride, he'd given a name to it,
3145 Because of King Charles' sword of which he'd heard:
†The pagan called his own sword Précïuse;
That was his cry upon the battlefield;
He has his knights all shout it in the fight.
He hangs about his neck a great broad shield
3150 With boss of gold and edged about with crystal,
Its neck strap is of fine embroidered silk.
The emir holds the lance he calls Maltét,
Its shaft is heavy, large any as club,
The iron tip alone a full mule's load.
3155 Now Baligant has mounted on his horse,
Marcule from o'er the sea his stirrup holds.
†Lord Baligant is built to ride a horse;
While slim his hips, his powerful ribs are wide,
His chest is deep and beautifully moulded;
3160 Wide are his shoulders, bright and fair his face,
Proud is his look, his head a crown of curls
Whiter by far than flowers of summertime;
A man of courage, proven many times.
God, what a noble lord were he but Christian!

3165 He spurs his horse; its blood spurts brightly forth;
     Forward he springs and leaps across a ditch
     Whose width a man might measure fifty feet.
     'Here is a man for holding provinces,'
     †The pagans cry, 'No Frank may fight with him
3170 But who must lose his life, will he or not.
     King Charles is mad not have taken flight!' AOI.

CCXXXII

     The emir is the picture of a lord;
     His beard is white, exactly like a flower,
     And he is wise in his religion's lore;
3175 In battle he is fierce and full of pride.
     His son Malpramis is most like a knight,
     In height and strength just like his ancestors;
     He says to his father, 'Sire, now let us ride!
     †I wonder if we shall see Charles this day?'
3180 Says Baligant, 'We shall, for he is brave.
     In many tales, great praise is told of him.
     †But here today he lacks his nephew Roland;
     He will not have the strength to stand us off.' AOI.

CCXXXIII

     'My good son Malpramis,' says Baligant,
3185 'The other day was killed the noble Roland,
     And Oliver, that brave and valiant man,
     With the twelve peers that King Charles loved so much
     And twenty thousand fighting knights of France.
     I have not much regard for all the others.'

CCXXXIV

3190 'Truly the emperor returns this way;
     My messenger, the Syrian, has told me.
     King Charles has formed ten very large divisions.
     He is most brave who sounds the olifant;
     His comrade answers with a trumpet blast;
3195 They ride right in the very foremost rank
     Together with them fifteen thousand Franks,
     †Young bachelors whom Charles calls warriors.

Behind these, just as many of the same.
Those men will fight with arrogance and pride.'
3200 Says Malpramis, 'Let me attack them first.' AOI.

CCXXXV

'Son Malpramis,' says Baligant to him,
'I grant you all that you have asked me here.
Make an attack against the French at once
And take with you Torleu, the Persian king,
3205 And Dapamort, the king from Lycia.
If you can but subdue the Frankish pride,
I shall give you that section of my land
From Cheriant up to the Val Marchis.'
The son replies, 'My lord, accept my thanks.'
3210 Then Malpramis rides forward, takes the gift
—It was the land which once was King Fleurit's.
†As it turned out, he never saw it more
And never took possession of his fief.

CCXXXVI

The emir Baligant rides through his host
3215 And his huge son follows where'er he goes.
The pagan kings Torleu and Dapamort
Soon form the army into thirty squadrons,
Each with enormous numbers in its ranks;
The smallest one has fifty thousand knights.
3220 The first contains the knights of Butenrot,
And, in the second, big-headed Micenes
Who, growing on their spines, straight up their backs,
Have bristles, and are hairy like a pig. AOI.

CCXXXVII

The third division holds the Nubles and Blos;
3225 The fourth division is of Bruns and Slavs;
†The fifth one is of other Slavs called Sorbres;
The sixth contains Armenians and Moors;
The seventh is of men of Jericho,
The eighth of Negroes and the ninth of Gros;
3230 The tenth is formed of men from strong Balide,
A people known for wickedness of mind. AOI.

CCXXXVIII

The emir Baligant swore mightily
By Mahomet himself and all his powers:
'King Charles of France is riding like one mad.
3235 We'll give him battle; unless he withdraws,
He'll never wear a golden crown again.'

CCXXXIX

Next they establish ten divisions more:
The first is formed of ugly Canaanites
Who have arrived across the Val Fuït;
3240 The next are Turks, and Persians form the third;
†The fourth composed of fiery Petchenegs,
The fifth division Soltras and Avars,
The sixth of Ormaleus and Eugiez,
The seventh, the army of Tsar Samuel,
3245 The eighth from Bruise, the ninth is of Clavers,
The tenth from Occian, that desert land,
A people who do not serve the Lord God
—You'll never hear of a more wicked race—
And on their bodies, skin as hard as iron,
3250 For which they shun helmet and hauberk both;
Vicious are they, and fierce upon the field. AOI.

CCXL

The emir then formed up ten more divisions.
The first was of the giants from Malpreis,
The next of Huns, the third Hungarians,
3255 The fourth from the great city of Baldise,
And the fifth of the men of Val Penuse;
†The sixth division has knights of Maruse,
The seventh of Lechs and men of Strymonis,
The eighth and ninth from Argoille and Clarbone,
3260 The tenth division, bearded men from Fronde,
There was a people who did not love God.
The Frankish history names thirty squadrons.
Vast are the armies where the trumpets sound;
The pagans ride along like valiant knights. AOI.

CCXLI

3265 The emir is a noble, powerful man;
  *He has his dragon staff borne on before
  With standards of Mahom and Tervagant,
  A statue of the wicked god Apollo.
  Around about him ride ten Canaanites,
3270 Who in their loudest voice cry out these words:
  'Let him who from our gods protection asks,
  Now pray and worship in humility!'
  The pagans now all bow their heads in prayer;
  They bend their shining helmets to the ground.
3275 The French say, 'You will die soon, infidels!
  This day may your destruction be complete!
  Oh Lord, our God, protect the life of Charles!
  †Let battle be declared now in his name!'   AOI.

CCXLII

  The emir is a man of greatest wisdom;
3280 He calls his son and the two kings to him
  And says, 'My noble lords, you'll ride in front
  And lead all my divisions on the field;
  But of the best I wish to keep back three:
  The Turk division, that of Ormaleus,
3285 And third will be the giants of Malpreis.
  The men of Occian will ride with me
  And will attack King Charles and his French knights.
  The emperor, if he should fight with me,
  Will surely lose the head from off his trunk.
3290 Let him be sure; his fate will be no less.' AOI.

CCXLIII

  How great the armies, beautiful the squadrons!
  Between them is no hill, nor vale, nor mound,
  Forest nor wood; no ambush hidden there.
  On open ground each army sees the other.
3295†Says Baligant, 'My people of the faith,
  Now ride and let us seek the battle out!'
  Amborre of Oluferne the ensign bears;
  The pagans shout and call out 'Précïuse!'
  The French reply, 'This day your loss be great!'

3300 In a loud voice they shout again 'Montjoie!'
The emperor now has his trumpets sound;
The olifant encourages them all.
The pagans say, 'Charles has a splendid host.
We'll have a terrible and stubborn fight.' Aoi.

CCXLIV

3305 Large is the plain and broad the countryside;
The sunshine glints on helmets decked with jewels,
Upon their shields and damascened hauberks,
On lances with their gonfanons attached;
The trumpets sound, their voices ringing high;
3310 Loud are the blasts blown on the olifant.
The emir Baligant calls to his brother
—He is Canabeus, King of Floredée,
Lord of the land as far as Val Sevrée—
And points out the divisions of King Charles:
3315 'Behold the pride of celebrated France!
The emperor rides very proudly on;
He is behind there, with that bearded host.
See how theyv'e put their beards outside their mail,
Beards just as white as snow that falls on frost;
3320 These men will strike with lances and with swords;
The battle will be bitter, hard-fought, long,
Such as no man has ever yet seen joined.'
Farther than one could throw a well-peeled rod,
Baligant rides ahead of his companions.
3325†He shouts encouragement to them and says,
'Follow me, brothers, I ride forward now!'
He brandishes the shaft of his great lance
And turns the iron point toward King Charles. Aoi.

CCXLV

King Charlemagne, as he sees the emir,
3330 The dragon staff, the ensign and the standard
—The infidels are present in such force,
They occupy the country on all sides
Except for that held by the emperor—
The king of France cries out in a loud voice,
3335 'My lords of France, you are the best of vassals;

You've fought so many battles in the field!
You see the pagans, foul and cowardly;
All their religion cannot help them now.
My lords, are we dismayed if they be many?
3340 Whoever will not ride with me, may go!'
Then with his spurs he urges on his horse,
And Tencendur rears up and makes four leaps.
The French reply, 'This king is brave indeed.
Ride on, brave knight, for none of us will fail you!'

CCXLVI

3345 The day is beautiful, the sun is bright,
The hosts magnificent, their numbers large,
The front divisions formed up for the fight.
The two French counts, Rabel and Guineman,
Let go the reins on their swift horses' backs,
3350 Spur forward eagerly; the Franks all charge
And with sharp lances ride to the attack. AOI.

CCXLVII

Count Rabel is a bold, courageous knight;
With fine gold spurs he urges on his horse
And rides to strike the Persian king, Torleu.
3355 Nor shield nor hauberk can withstand the blow
As Rabel stabs him with his gilded lance
And knocks him dead onto a little bush.
The French say, 'May the Lord God help us here!
King Charles is right; we must not fail him now.' AOI.

CCXLVIII

3360 Then Guineman attacks the Lycian king;
First smashing through his ornamented shield,
Then tearing through the armoured leather tunic,
He shoves his pennant clear into his body,
Striking him dead whoe'er may laugh or weep.
3365 Seeing this blow, the men of France cry out,
'Do not hang back, my lords, but strike hard blows!
†Against these pagans, Charles is in the right!
God has charged us with rendering true judgement.'
                                                    AOI.

CCXLIX

Malpramis sits upon a pure white horse.
3370 He throws himself amid the Frankish press,
Striking out regularly as he rides
And often piles one dead man on the last.
The emir Baligant is first to shout,
'My barons, I have cared for you so long;
3375 See how my son goes seeking out King Charles,
Challenging many brave men with his arms.
No better vassal than he do I ask.
With your sharp lances, ride to help him now!'
On hearing this, the pagans all move forward;
3380 They strike hard blows; the fight is general.
Now is the battle fearful, grievous, costly;
Not one such fought before nor since that time. Aoi.

CCL

Great are the armies, proud the companies,
Every division now has joined the battle.
3385 Pagans attack and strike prodigious blows.
How many lances broken now in two!
How many shattered shields and damaged hauberks!
You would have seen the ground all strewn with bodies,
The tender grass, so green upon the field,
3390†Red with the blood that flowed forth from their
       wounds.
The emir Baligant calls to his knights:
'Strike hard, my lords, upon this Christian host!'
Hard is the battle, stubbornly contested;
None like it fought, either before or since.
3395 No truce will be agreed on, short of death. Aoi.

CCLI

The emir Baligant calls to his host,
'Brothers, attack! You came for that alone!
For I shall give you lovely, noble women,
As well as privileges, fiefs, and lands.'
3400 The pagans say, 'Now we must do our best!'
They shatter lances, striking mighty blows;
Then draw more than a hundred thousand swords.

How terrible the fighting hand to hand!
*But one who watches would be in the battle. Aoi.

CCLII

3405 The emperor then calls upon the French:
'My noble lords, I love and trust in you.
You've fought so many battles for my sake
And conquered kingdoms and brought low their kings!
Well do I know I owe you all rewards
3410 From my own hands in lands and other wealth.
Avenge your sons, your brothers and your heirs
Killed just the other day at Rencesvals!
Be sure, my cause is just against the pagans!'
The French reply, 'My lord, you speak the truth!'
3415 Some twenty thousand knights he has with him,
And all together now they pledge their faith:
They will not fail for fear of pain or death;
Not one but who will lay on with his lance.
Then with their swords they straightaway attack;
3420 The battle now is fearful, terrible. Aoi.

CCLIII

While Malpramis is riding through the field,
Making great slaughter of the men of France,
Duke Naimes is keeping his fierce eyes on him,
And then attacks him like a valiant man.
3425 He strikes him high upon the pagan's shield,
Destroys the decoration of his mail,
And rams the yellow pennon in his body
Laying him dead mid seven hundred others.

CCLIV

King Canabeus, brother of Baligant,
3430 Then urges his horse forward with the spur;
The pagan draws his crystal-pommelled sword
And strikes Duke Naimes atop his princely helm;
He manages to shatter half one side
And cut five laces with the blade of steel.
3435 The chain mail hood protects Naimes not a bit;

The blade goes through his cap into his flesh
And cuts a slice that falls upon the ground.
The blow was terrible; the duke is dazed.
He would have fainted then, had God not helped;
3440 Naimes flings his arms around his horse's neck;
But had the Saracen attacked again,
That noble vassal would have died at once.

CCLV

Duke Naimes is in most agonizing pain.
3445 The pagan makes all haste to strike him down.
Charles cries, 'Wretch! Woe that you laid hands on
    him!'
And strikes him with great courage, strength and skill;
Crushing the pagan's shield against his heart,
He tears apart the hauberk's chain mail hood
3450 And strikes him dead; empty his saddle now.

CCLVI

Great is the grief of Charlemagne the king,
Seeing Duke Naimes before him, badly wounded,
His bright blood dripping down on the green grass.
The emperor says to him quietly,
3455 'My fair lord Naimes, now ride here by my side.
The wretch is dead who was attacking you;
I stabbed him once for all with my own lance.'
The duke replies, 'My lord, I give my word:
If I live on, you shall have great reward.'
3460 In love and trust the two are reunited;
With them there are some twenty thousand French;
Not one but who attacks, fights man to man. Aoi.

CCLVII

The emir rides across the battlefield
And so comes to attack Count Guineman.
3465 Smashing the Christian's white shield on his heart,
He tears the panels of his coat of mail,
Severing ribs from body on both sides,
And strikes him dead on his swift-running horse.
Then the emir kills Gebuin and Lorain,

3470 Richard the Old, lord of the Norman knights.
The pagans cry out, 'Powerful Précïuse!'
Attack, my lords, for it is our defence!' AOI.

CCLVIII

Could one then have but seen the Arab knights!
The knights of Occiant, Argoille and Bascle!
3475 They fight hard with their spears and hand to hand,
But still the French have no desire to flee,
And many die on both sides of the field.
The battle rages till the evening comes.
Great are the losses of the Frankish lords.
3480 Sorrow will mount e'er it be broken off. AOI.

CCLIX

Both French and Arabs fight their very best,
Shatter their lances and their burnished spears.
Whoever saw those crushed and battered shields,
Or heard the ring of steel on shining mail,
3485 Or grating blows of swords on helmet tops,
Or saw knights topple from their horses' backs,
Or heard men screaming, dying on the ground,
He would remember pain unparalleled.
This battle asks the utmost of endurance.
3490 The emir Baligant calls on Apollo,
And Tervagant and Mahomet as well:
'My lords, my gods, I have served you so well;
I'll make you images of finest gold.' AOI.

† . . . .
3495 His favourite, Gemalfin, appears before him;
He brings the emir evil news and says:
'My lord, events are going ill today:
You've lost your son Malpramis on the field
And Canabeus your brother has been killed;
3500 A French knight came off well in both encounters;
I think the emperor was one of them.
With his huge build he looks a noble lord;
He has a beard as white as April flowers.'
Lord Baligant bows down his helm at this,
3505 Then afterwards he drops his face in grief,

Thinking to die at once from such great woe.
He sends for Jangleu from beyond the sea.

CCLX

The emir says, 'Jangleu, step forward here!
You are a worthy man and very wise
3510 And I have always yielded to your counsel.
How do you judge between the Franks and Arabs?
Will our men have the victory in the field?'
Jangleu replies, 'You are doomed, Baligant.
Your gods can give you no protection now.
3515 King Charles is proud and fierce, valiant his men,
I have not seen a host so bellicose.
But, call upon your lords of Occiant,
Turks and Enfruns, giants, Arabians!
Seek no more to delay that which must be.'

CCLXI

3520 The emir puts his beard out in plain sight,
A beard as white as is the hawthorn flower.
Whate'er befalls, he does not wish to hide.
He puts a shining trumpet to his lips
And sounds a clear note that his pagans hear;
3525 Throughout the battlefield, his companies rally.
The men of Occiant both bray and whinny;
The men of Argoille yap and bark like dogs.
Then they attack the Franks so recklessly,
They break and separate their thickest ranks.
3530 In this charge they kill seven thousand men.

CCLXII

The count Oger was never cowardly;
A better vassal never wore a hauberk.
When Oger sees the French divisions break,
He calls to him Duke Tierri of Argonne,
3535 Godefroy d'Anjou and the count Jozeran,
And with fierce pride he then harangues King Charles:
'Look at the pagans killing all your men!
Please God that you may wear the crown no more
If you do not charge now, avenge your shame!'

3540 Not one man can reply a single word.
Forward they spur, letting their horses run.
They will attack the pagans where they find them.

CCLXIII

King Charlemagne is fighting well and hard Aoi.
With Naimes the duke, Count Oger of Denmark,
3545 And Godefroy of Anjou who holds the banner.
Count Oger is the bravest of the brave;
He spurs his horse, letting it run full speed,
Charging so hard the dragon standard bearer
That Amborre falls most heavily before him,
3550 And both the standard and the ensign too.
When Baligant sees his gonfanon fall,
And Mahomet's own standard overthrown,
Then he perceives some measure of the truth
That he is wrong and Charlemagne is right;
3555†The Saracens then lose enthusiasm.
King Charles calls loudly on his countrymen:
'Speak! Will you help me now for God's own sake?'
The Franks reply, 'You do not have to ask!
Let him be cursed who does not fight his best!' Aoi.

CCLXIV

3560 The daylight fades, passing to evening dusk;
Both Franks and pagans fight on with their swords.
Most valiant those who brought the hosts together;
Their battle cries they never have forgotten:
The emir Baligant shouts, 'Précïuse!'
3565 And Charles his famous battle cry 'Montjoie!'
They recognize each other's loud, clear voice
And, in the middle of the field, they meet.
Riding to the attack, each strikes the other
A lance blow on his decorated shield;
3570 Each shield is smashed beneath its ample boss,
Each hauberk's lower panels torn away,
But neither wounds the other in the flesh.
They break each other's cinches, spill their saddles,
The two kings fall and tumble to the ground.
3575 Quickly they rise upon their feet again

And each one draws his sword most valiantly.
This single combat cannot be averted;
Without a dead man it cannot be finished. Aoi.

CCLXV

King Charles of lovely France is powerful, brave;
3580 The emir does not stand in awe of him.
They show the naked edges of their swords
And strike great blows, each on the other's shield;
They split the leather hides, the double frames;
The nails fall out, they smash the boss to bits;
3585 Then, shieldless, strike upon the hauberk's mail
And sparks of fire fly up from the bright helms.
This single combat cannot ever end,
Till one of them will recognize his wrong. Aoi.

CCLXVI

The emir says, 'King Charles, now give a thought!
3590 Take my advice and tell me you repent!
I know that you have killed my son today,
And wrongly challenge me for my own land.
Become my vassal and this fief is yours!
Come and serve me from here through all the east!'
3595 Charles says, 'I look on that as degradation.
I must grant neither peace nor love to pagans.
Receive that faith God has prepared for us,
The faith of Christ and I shall love you ever!
Serve and believe the Mightiest of Kings!'
3600 Says Baligant, 'Your argument is useless.'
They both return to fighting with their swords. Aoi.

CCLXVII

The emir is a man of strength and courage;
He strikes Charles on his helm of burnished steel,
Splitting and denting it upon his head,
3605 Striking the sword through his thick, curly hair,
Slicing off flesh a hand's breadth wide and more.
Charles' skull is all exposed beneath the wound.
He staggers and he very nearly falls.
God does not wish that he be killed or conquered.

3610 Saint Gabriel comes to the emperor's side
And asks him, 'Mighty king, what are you doing?'

CCLXVIII

When King Charles hears the angel's holy voice,
Because of it he has no fear of death.
Both strength and consciousness return to him.
3615 He strikes the emir with the sword of France;
He splits his helmet where the jewels flash,
Cuts through his head, spilling the emir's brains,
On through his face down to the snow-white beard,
Striking him dead beyond recovery.
3620 Charles shouts 'Montjoie!' to claim his victory.
On hearing this, Duke Naimes comes riding up;
He holds Tencendur while the king mounts up.
The pagans fly; God will not let them stay.
†Now can the French do what they have long wanted.

CCLXIX

3625 The pagans now are fleeing as God wills;
The Franks pursue them with the emperor.
The king says, 'Now, my Lords, avenge your grief!
Lighten your hearts and soothe your passions too!
Because this very morn I saw you weep.'
3630 The French reply, 'Sire, we have need of this!'
Each one strikes all the blows that he can manage,
And few escape among the fleeing band.

CCLXX

The heat is great and the dust billows up.
The pagans flee, the French harassing them.
3635 The chase lasts all the way to Sarragoce.
Queen Bramimonde has gone up to her tower,
Together with her clerks and canons both
Of that false faith which God has never loved;
They have no orders and no tonsured heads.
3640 When she beholds the Saracens defeated,
In a loud voice she cries, 'Help us, Mahom!
Ah, noble king, now all our men are vanquished,
Even the emir killed in deepest shame!'

When Marsilie hears, he turns toward the wall;
3645 His eyes are full of tears, his head sunk low;
He dies of grief amid calamity,
And gives his soul to devils out of hell. Aoi.

CCLXXI

Some pagans dead, the rest of them in flight,
Now Charles has won a total victory.
3650 He's broken down the gates of Saragoce,
Sure now they will no longer be defended.
He takes the citadel; his army enters;
The victors sleep that night within its walls.
The king with the white beard is proud and haughty;
3655 Queen Bramimonde surrenders him her towers,
Ten larger towers and fifty smaller ones.
He whom the Lord God helps, performs great deeds.

CCLXXII

All daylight passes and the night grows dark;
Bright is the moon, the stars are twinkling.
3660 The emperor has taken Saragoce.
A thousand French search well throughout the town
In all the synagogues and mosques as well;
With iron hammers, hatchets in their hands,
They smash the images and all the idols.
3665 No sorcery or fraud will here remain.
The king believes in God, desires His service;
The bishops therefore bless some holy water
And lead the pagans to the baptistery.
If now a single one opposes Charles,
3670 He has him hanged or burned or killed outright.
More than a hundred thousand are baptized
True Christians, with the exception of the queen;
She will be led a captive to sweet France.
Charles would convert her with both love and kindness.

CCLXXIII

3675 The night is past and the bright day returns.
Charles garrisons the towers of Saragoce,
Leaving a thousand veteran warrior knights

To guard the city for the emperor.
The king mounts on his horse with all his men
3680 And Bramimonde whom he takes as a captive,
Though he intends to do her only good.
So they return with gladness and rejoicing.
They pass Nerbone with a great show of force
And then come to the city of Bordeaux.
3685 Upon the altar of Saint Severin
Charles puts the olifant, filled with gold coins;
The pilgrims who pass by will see it there.
They pass across the Gironde in great ships
And up to Blaive Charles takes his nephew's corpse
3690 With that of Oliver, his noble comrade
And Turpin too, the wise and brave archbishop.
Within white coffins King Charles has them placed;
The barons lie at rest in Saint Romain.
*The Franks commend them to the names of God.
3695 Charles rides on through the valleys and the hills;
He will not rest until he reaches Aix;
He rides till he sets foot before his door.
When Charlemagne is in his proud, high palace,
By his own messengers he sends for judges,
3700 Bavarians, Saxons, Frisians and Lorraines;
He sends for Germans, men from Burgundy,
Men of Poitou, Normans and Bretons both,
And for the wisest of the men of France.
For now begins the trial of Ganelon.

CCLXXIV

3705 The emperor has now returned from Spain
And come to Aix, the foremost seat of France.
He mounts up to the great hall of the palace.
Before him Alde appears, a lovely maid,
And says to him, 'Where is the captain Roland,
3710 Who swore to come and take me as his wife?'
Charles feels the heaviness of grief and pain;
Tears fill his eyes, he tugs at his white beard:
'Sister, dear friend, you ask about the dead.
I give you in exchange a higher match:
3715 Louis; I know no better one in France.

He is my son and he will have my crown.'
But Alde replies, 'I find these words repugnant.
May it not please God nor his saints and angels
That after Roland's death I should live on.'
3720 And, turning pale, she falls at King Charles' feet.
In that same breath she dies. God keep her soul!
The French knights mourn the maid and weep for her.

CCLXXV

Beautiful Alde has gone to meet her end.
But the king thinks that she has only fainted.
3725 The emperor feels pity and he weeps;
He takes her by the hand and raises her,
Her head is hanging over on her shoulder.
When the king sees that he has found her dead,
At once he sends word for four countesses;
3730 Fair Alde is borne within a convent's walls.
All night they watch around her until dawn,
Bury her fittingly beside the altar.
The king gives great endowment to the convent. Aoi.

CCLXXVI

The emperor has now returned to Aix.
3735 The felon Ganelon, in iron chains,
Stands in the citadel before the palace.
The servants have attached him to a post
And also tied his hands with deerhide thongs.
They beat him well with gambrils and with sticks.
3740 The man has not deserved a different fate.
There in great pain does he await his trial.

CCLXXVII

Now it is written in the ancient tale
That King Charles sent for men from many lands.
They are assembled at Aix-la-Chapelle.
3745 Sharp at high noon—it is a great feast day,
The feast, say some, of my lord Saint Silvester—
Begins the trial, with speeches and rebuttal,
Of Ganelon who has committed treason.
Into his presence King Charles has him dragged. Aoi.

CCLXXVIII

3750 'My lords and barons,' says King Charlemagne,
       'Give me true judgement on Count Ganelon!
       The count was in the host I took to Spain;
       He took from me my twenty thousand French,
       My nephew Roland, whom you'll see no more,
3755 The brave and noble knight, Count Oliver;
       The twelve peers he betrayed for gold and wealth.'
       'Now judge me guilty if I hide all this,'
       †Says Ganelon. 'Roland wronged me through greed.
       For that I sought to bring him pain and death.
3760 But in this act, I shall admit no treason.'
       The French reply, 'Now let us hold a council.'

CCLXXIX

       Count Ganelon stands there before the king;
       Robust his form, handsome of hue his face;
       If only loyal, he would look most noble.
3765 He looks upon the French and all his judges;
       With him are thirty of his relatives.
       Ganelon cries aloud in a great voice:
       'Now hear me, barons, for the love of God!
       My lords, I was in Charles' own host in Spain,
3770 And served him there with loyalty and love.
       His nephew had conceived a hatred for me
       And nominated me for death and pain:
       I was ambassador to King Marsilie.
       Through my own wisdom, I came safely through;
3775 *I had declared a feud with mighty Roland,
       Count Oliver and all of their companions;
       Charles heard it, and his noble barons too.
       I am avenged; but treason it is not.'
       The Franks reply, 'Let us take counsel now.'

CCLXXX

3780 When Ganelon sees that his trial is starting,
       He has thirty relations at his side;
       And there is one to whom the others listen:

Lord Pinabel of Castel de Sorence.
He speaks well and knows how to give good counsel,
3785 A valiant man who can protect himself. Aoi.

CCLXXXI

†Ganelon says, 'I place great faith in you.
Protect me now from accusation, death!'
Says Pinabel, 'I shall be your protection.
No Frank alive will sentence you to hang
3790 But that, should King Charles bring us two together,
I'll make him disavow it with my sword.'
Ganelon kneels down at his feet in thanks.

CCLXXXII

Bavarians and Saxons are in council,
With men of Poitou, Normans and the French,
3795 Among them also Alemans and Germans.
The men of the Auvergne show most compassion;
Because of Pinabel they hold their peace.
Men tell each other, 'It is best to stop.
Let us suspend the trial and ask the king
3800 That he acquit Count Ganelon this time;
Then let him serve the king in faith and love.
Roland is dead; you will see him no more;
He will not be brought back by gold or wealth.
He would be mad who'd fight about this now!'
3805 Not one of them but grants this and agrees
Except Tierri, Godefroy of Anjou's brother. Aoi.

CCLXXXIII

The barons now return to Charlemagne
And say to him, 'My lord and king, we ask
That you will now acquit Count Ganelon.
3810 Let him serve you henceforth in faith and love.
Let the count live; he is of noble birth;
†His death is not the price of Roland's life,
Nor yet for wealth may we recover him.'
*Charles says, 'You all are criminals to me!' Aoi.

CCLXXXIV

3815 When Charles sees that his barons have proved false,
  †For a long time he sits, his head bowed down.
  In grief he calls himself unhappy wretch.
  But then before him stands a knight, Tierri,
  The brother of Duke Godefroy of Anjou.
3820 His build is spare and slender, even slim,
  Black is his hair and somewhat dark his face;
  One could not call him big, nor yet too small.
  He speaks with courtesy to Charlemagne:
  'My lord the king, do not lament this way.
3825 You know that I have served you long and well.
  For family's sake, I must support your cause.
  However Roland may have wronged the count,
  †A man's first duty is his sovereign's service.
  Having betrayed that, Ganelon is guilty.
3830 Against you he is perjured, compromised;
  Hence my decision that he should be hanged
  †And given over to both pain and death
  Just like the felon who commits a crime.
  If any kin of his give me the lie,
3835 With this my sword that I have girded on
  I stand prepared to uphold my decision.'
  The Franks are shouting, 'Lord, you've spoken well!'

CCLXXXV

  Lord Pinabel then steps before the king,
  A strong and valiant man, both large and fast;
3840 The man he strikes has little time to live.
  He says to Charles, 'My lord, this is your court.
  Give orders that this noise and uproar cease.
  I see that Tierri here has given judgement;
  I call it false and I shall fight with him.'
3845 He puts his right glove in the emperor's hand.
  Charles says, 'I ask good hostages for you,'
  And thirty loyal relatives all swear.
    *Charles says to them, 'I give him to your care,'
  And has them closely guarded till the trial. Aoi.

CCLXXXVI

3850 When Tierri sees a combat will be held,
He offers his right glove to Charlemagne.
The king secures Tierri with hostages,
Then has four benches brought into the square.
The adversaries take their seats on them,
3855 Summoned to combat by their peers' decision;
Oger of Denmark sets forth the detail;
Then they ask for their horses and their arms.

CCLXXXVII

Because they are appointed to do battle, Aoi.
Both have confession, absolution, blessing;
3860 They each hear masses and communicate
And make large contributions to the church.
Then both of them return before the king.
Their spurs are fitted firmly on their feet,
They wear their shining hauberks, strong and light,
3865 Their gleaming helmets laced upon their heads,
Their golden-pommelled swords are girded on,
Around their necks the quartered shields are hung,
In their right hands they hold their sharpened lances;
At last they mount upon their swift war horses.
3870 A hundred thousand knights are weeping now
With pity for both Roland and Tierri.
And God alone is sure how it will end.

CCLXXXVIII

The field beneath the town of Aix is wide;
The combat of the two knights is prepared,
3875 Both of them worthy men, loyal and brave,
And both their horses swift and fleet of foot.
They spur them forward, letting go the reins,
And with great strength they ride to the attack,
Shatter, completely crush each other's shields,
3880 Tear through the hauberks, break the saddle girths;
The bows turn as the saddles fly to earth.
A hundred thousand men are watching, weeping.

CCLXXXIX

Now both the knights find themselves on the ground.
AOI.

Quickly they leap on to their feet again.
3885 Lord Pinabel, though big, is light and fast;
They seek each other out without their mounts.
Now with their swords whose hilts are purest gold,
They fight and strike each at the other's helm,
The blows enough to cut a helm in two.
3890 The knights of France lament and mourn aloud.
'Ah God,' cries Charles. 'Make clear the right in this!'

CCXC

Says Pinabel, 'Tierri, yield to me now!
I'll be your vassal in both love and faith,
And at your pleasure give you all I have;
3895 But reconcile the king and Ganelon.'
Tierri replies, 'That I cannot consider.
I'd be a traitor if I granted that!
Let God decide the right between us now!' AOI.

CCXCI

Says Tierri, 'Pinabel, noble and brave,
3900 You are both large and strong and muscled well;
Your peers know well your loyalty and courage;
As for this battle, let it stop right here,
And I shall make your peace with Charlemagne.
To Ganelon such justice shall be done,
3905 No day will pass men will not speak of it.'
Says Pinabel, 'May God forbid me that!
I shall uphold my family honour fully.
I'll not give in to any mortal man;
I'd rather die than suffer such reproach.'
3910 They take up fighting with their swords again,
Striking great blows upon their gilded helms
Till the bright sparks fly upwards to the sky.
It is impossible to part them now;
The combat cannot end without a death. AOI.

CCXCII

3915 Great is the prowess of Count Pinabel;
He strikes Tierri on his Provençal helm;
The sparks that fly off set the grass alight.
Pinabel swings the steel sword point at him,
†Bringing it down to cut across his forehead
3920 And then slash down across Lord Tierri's face.
His right cheek is all bloodied from the blow,
His hauberk slashed and open to his waist.
But God prevents his being cut down dead. Aoi.

CCXCIII

Tierri sees he is wounded in the face,
3925 The red blood falling to the meadow grass.
He strikes his adversary on the helm,
Down to the nose guard splits and shatters it,
Scattering far and wide the champion's brains.
He raised his sword and struck him dead to earth.
3930 With one blow is the single combat won.
The French cry, 'God has made a miracle!
It is but just that Ganelon be hanged
With all his family that upheld his cause!' Aoi.

CCXCIV

When Lord Tierri had gained the victory,
3935 The emperor Charlemagne came up to him
With forty of his barons round about,
Among them Naimes and Oger of Denmark,
Godefroy of Anjou and Willalme de Blaive.
The king has taken Tierri in his arms
3940 And wiped his face with his great marten furs;
Putting them down, he wraps him in still others.
Then very gently they disarm the knight.
They have him mount on an Arabian mule
And, with great joy and knightly pomp, return.
3945 Coming to Aix, they dismount in the square.
Now will begin the felons' execution.

CCXCV

Charles calls upon his nobles, counts and dukes:
'What is your counsel on my prisoners?
For Ganelon they came to these assizes;
3950 They stood as hostages for Pinabel.'
The French reply, 'Not one of them should live!'
The king commands an officer, Basbrun:
'Go, hang them all upon the gallows tree!
And by my beard whose hair is white as snow,
3955†If one escapes, then count yourself as dead.'
He answers, 'What would I do but my duty?'
And with a hundred guards, marches them out.
There are full thirty of them that are hanged.
Let traitors and their fellows suffer death! Aoi.

CCXCVI

3960 And then return Bavarians, Alemans,
The Poitevins, Bretons and Normans too.
More than the rest, the French are in accord
That Ganelon should die in agony.
Four war horses are then led out in front;
3965 They tie him to them by the feet and hands.
The horses are high-spirited and fast;
Four soldiers take charge of the horses' heads.
Beside a stream that flows amid the field,
Count Ganelon is sent to his destruction:
3970 His ligaments are stretched out inch by inch;
His legs and arms are torn off one by one;
On the green grass spatters his bright red blood;
And Ganelon dies like a wicked traitor.
It is not just that traitors live to boast.

CXCVII

3975 When Charles the emperor has been avenged,
He calls together bishops from all France,
And from Bavaria and Germany:
'There is a noble captive in my house
And she has heard such sermons and examples,
3980 She wishes to believe the Christian faith.

Baptize her now that God may have her soul.'
They say, 'By godmothers let it be done,
†By ladies who are trustworthy and noble.'
Great is the gathering beside the baths;
3985 They give the Queen of Spain her baptism.
They choose for her the name of Juliane.
She is a Christian of sincere conviction.

CCXCVIII

Now Charles has seen the sentence carried out,
And his great anger is appeased and calmed.
3990 He has had Bramimonde baptized a Christian.
The daylight passes and night settles in;
The king lies down in his high-vaulted chamber.
Saint Gabriel comes from God to speak to him:
'Charles, summon up the armies of your realm!
3995 You'll go in force into the land of Bire
Where you will help King Vivien at Imphe,
The citadel the pagans are besieging.
The Christians cry aloud and call on you.'
The emperor has no desire to go.
4000 'God,' says the king, 'how wearisome my life!'
Charlemagne weeps and pulls at his white beard.
*Ci falt la geste que Turoldus declinet.

NOTES AND GLOSSARY

NOTES TO THE TEXT

Notes marked in the text with an asterisk are of general interest to readers; those marked with a dagger are of special interest to readers working with the original.

9. Aoi is an unsolved mystery. Occurring at the end of some *laisses* and (probably through scribal error) at the beginning of a few, it has been thought a musical notation for the guidance of a minstrel or an exclamation of dramatic import. André de Mandach ('The so-called Aoi in the *Chanson de Roland*,' *Symposium* XI (1957) 303–15) says that it is a corruption of the letters 'Am' (Amen). A survey and attempted solution is offered by Herman J. Green, 'The Etymology of Aoi and Ae, *Modern Language Notes* 85, No. 4 (1970), 593–8.

12. *Bloi* (<Germanic *blaudhi*?) might have meant 'livid' and hence 'blue' or 'yellow' in Old French.

42. Literally, 'the sons of our wives', i.e., our legitimate heirs; a considerable sacrifice on the part of the Saracens.

50. *Franc* (Franks) and *Franceis* (Frenchmen) are used interchangeably throughout the poem with the exception of v. 396, q.v.

69. Literally translated here, *felun* usually means 'wicked' but is used frequently to refer to the Saracens. The sense is: 'of the most typically pagan from the Christian point of view'.

77. This literally translated line underscores the seriousness of the Saracen dilemma. The ambassadors have no need of their king's traditional encouragement to carry out their assignment.

243. The simple formula *Dient Franceis* ('The French say') indicates here, as in vv. 192, 278, and elsewhere, an approving decision on the part of the council. Similarly, v. 263 demonstrates their unwillingness to speak as, policy decided, they leave the implementation to the king. See v. 321 for confirmation.

247. The right-hand glove symbolizes the power of the emperor, the staff his authority.

270. The word *semblant* means both 'appearance' and 'attitude'. We have tried to render the double meaning.

326. This is the formal challenge which establishes a feud between Roland and his followers on one hand and Ganelon and his followers on the other. The fact of having openly challenged Roland is referred to by Ganelon in vv. 3775–8 as part of his defence.

335. Old French *message* can mean 'mission, embassy' or 'ambassador, envoy'. We have not succeeded in rendering the obvious ambiguity which makes Ganelon's reply all the more threatening.

350. Placing a comma before *ber* in Whitehead's text thus: *Tant mar fustes, ber*, allows our translation, literally 'In an evil hour (i.e., How unfortunate that . . .) you were [born], noble knight!'.

396. We interpret *la franceise gent* as meaning the 20,000 knights from French territory, loyal to their compatriot Roland.

441. Literally 'he has changed colour'. See also v. 485, where the verb is *esculurer*, variously translated as 'to become highly coloured, flushed' (Bédier) and 'lose colour' (Whitehead).

456. The Old French is obscure but seems to mean 'I must endure or tolerate it'.

494. Literally, 'he will not love (i.e., be on friendly terms with) me otherwise'. The expression is formal, almost diplomatic, and we translate freely. Cf. v. 306.

495. The text is not completely clear, but this seems to be the Caliph's son. Perhaps he is the same hothead we find in *laisse* LXIX.

520. Other examples will be found in the poem, but *laisses* XL–XLII offer the clearest example of the use of *laisses similaires*, two or three stanzas repeating the same basic material but with small and often significant changes. Robert A. Hall ('Linguistic Strata in the *Chanson de Roland*',

Romance Philology XIII (1959), 156–61) sees here an indication of the fusion of two versions of the poem. The phenomenon appears functional, however, in the addition of specific detail.

604. The end of this verse is missing in the ms. We translate freely from Whitehead's suggestion: 'Counsel [of which one is not sure] is of no advantage'.

611. Tervagant is apparently supposed by the author to be just one more pagan god among many. Mediaeval Christian authors were either unaware of or uninterested by the monotheism of Islam.

616. Ganelon's statement (*Ben seit vostre comant*) is obscure. We follow Bédier's suggestion (*Commentaire*, pp. 147–8).

618. Whitehead's emendation of this line is not what we translate. We translate the ms (*Icie en vait al reil Marsiliun*) quite literally.

621. Bédier (*Commentaire*, pp. 206–7) suggests that Valdabrun is obliquely offering a sword *and* a thousand gold *manguns* (a Saracen coin), adding that the fact is confirmed by v. 1570. We follow one sense of the ms and let the reader decide.

711. The last half of this line is missing in the ms. We offer an alternative to a blank space.

727. We adopt Bédier's view (*Commentaire*, p. 207) that this is a bear, not a boar. The sense seems supported by the *brohun* in v. 2557.

761. The tone of this *laisse* conflicts sharply with that of the preceding one. We see in these two *laisses* first the public chivalrous reply and then a private reply by Roland to his stepfather.

849–50. Some of the Saracen titles of nobility and rank defy translation. *Amiraill* roughly equals 'emir'. Others, such as *amirafle* or *amurafle*, *almacur*, *cuntur* are generally left in the original. In v. 850, *cuntur* is translated as 'lesser lord'. The general effect is, one hopes, as exotic for the modern reader as it probably was for the mediaeval audience.

999. The *gonfanon* is a standard belonging to a noble or king and generally attached to a lance or pole. It may be roughly triangular in shape and may be decorated with streamers (vv. 1157–8). We translate variously as 'standard', 'battle flag' or simply use *gonfanon*. The standard bearer is called the *gonfanoner* (v. 106). See the note to v. 3266.

1032. The word *safrez* is mysterious. We accept White-head's 'damascened'. Other notions are 'painted in yellow enamel' or 'blue-bordered'.

1070. The ivory horn is called the *olifant* (<Latin *elephantum*).

1078. Numbers in mediaeval texts tend to be round and exaggerated. The ms says that Roland struck *mil colps e .vii. cenz* (i.e., 1700 blows). The effect is to indicate that he struck more blows than one could count. Today we would say a 'million' or a 'billion'.

1082. Literally, 'I can find no blame in that' (*D'ico ne sai jo blasme*). *Ico* refers back to the idea of blowing the horn as Oliver suggested.

1092. Literally, 'The emperor loves us more for our striking well'.

1123. The line is one syllable short in the ms but makes perfect sense in conjunction with the previous line.

1144. Literally, 'they are all prepared for battle'.

1158. Whitehead suggests *lengues* ('streamers') instead of the ms *renges* ('baldric'?).

1165. *Le pas tenant* is variously interpreted as 'slowly' and 'keep in line'. Since the preceding *suef* can mean 'easily', 'slowly', we choose the second possibility.

1181. *Montjoie!* is Charlemagne's battle cry. It is supposed to be derived from the pilgrims' shout on seeing the Mons Gaudia from which they caught a first glimpse of Jerusalem (according to Whitehead), Rome (according to

Jenkins). No one knows its origin; not even the author of the *Roland* who explains his own theory in vv. 2507–10.

1185. Literally, 'what other thing would they do?' the idea being that duty calls them irresistibly.

1204. The expression *pleine sa hanste* occurs frequently in the battle scenes. Various translations have been offered and we have been eclectic in our choice of them: 'the full length of his lance', 'with lance outstretched'.

1262. A *denier* was a coin of very small value, being one-twelfth of a *sou*.

1360. Literally, 'What are you doing?'

1387. The two Christian knights do not purposely attack the pagan at the same time. They charged from different parts of the field, arriving simultaneously.

1448. Whitehead suggests the possibility of a lacuna in the ms at this point; our translation simply follows the ms without difficulty.

1486. Turpin is not calling Abisme a coward. Jenkins (p. 114) puts it well: 'the archbishop is communing with himself, and is perhaps not unaffected by the look of the fell Saracen'.

1502–3. The ms is unclear here about who actually gave the shield to Abisme. We follow Bédier (*Commentaire*, pp. 215–16) who interprets the devil as intermediary.

1509. Evidently this archbishop's crozier is a lance.

1529. See laisse XLIX for the incident referred to.

1543. It is bizarre but true that the Saracens sometimes refer to each other as 'pagans'.

1653. We follow Whitehead's numbering of the *laisses* and preservation of the order of the ms. See his note to v. 1653 and M. K. Pope, *Medium Aevum*, I (1932), 81–6.

1666. We leave the line blank at the apparent lacuna in order to keep the line numbering.

1807. Whitehead's spelling of the first word of this line should be *esclargiz* as his glossary confirms. The line is unclear and we translate freely.

1843. Jenkins (p. 139) interprets the beard worn outside the armour as a sign of defiance.

1848–50. We interpret this as a typical reflection of one of the French knights riding to Roland's aid.

1863. We translate *pur mei* ambiguously as 'on my account' to reflect the ambiguity of the Old French which can mean 'because of me' or 'for me'. The question is: to what extent does Roland realize or accept responsibility for the loss of his 20,000 knights?

1894. Literally, 'without [doing] any other harm'. A single blow was sufficient.

2034. Literally, 'wherever he may go'. Bédier prefers to read 'lean' (*pencher*); either seems adequate.

2055. Editors believe that a lacuna exists in the ms after this verse. Bédier (*Commentaire*, pp. 190–2) reviews the possibilities.

2075. Whitehead prints the fifteen-syllable line as two defective lines; we reduce 2075 and 2075a rather freely to one line.

2172. We translate freely, adding 'cutting . . . off'.

2192. Literally, at his 'knees'.

2357. Literally, 'he ran beneath'.

2369–72. Our translation differs from Whitehead's provisional translation in his glossary which does not account for the first line of this *Confiteor*.

2414. The ms has *cum* before *hom*.

2445. Whitehead translates 'have made them turn and flee'. We accept Bédier's emendation from *unt lur* to *lur unt* and translate accordingly.

2453. Literally, 'quickly he commanded him'.

2469. Literally, 'but they have no protection'.

2565. Editors usually give 'beyond' for *ultre*.

2616. As Jenkins points out in his note to this line, the text may mean that Baligant lived to a greater age than Homer or Virgil, or that he was their contemporary and outlived them. The effect is to ascribe great age to the emir and thus pair him suitably with Charlemagne.

2625. The translation cannot distinguish exactly the different types of warships in the pagan fleet.

2633. The carbuncle (Latin *carbunculus*, 'tumour', 'red object' and originally 'a live coal') was believed to shine at night.

2697. Literally, 'whom they do not have at all'.

2743. Literally, 'You see that I am harassed unto death'.

2837. We reproduce Jenkins' note to this line: 'Baligant means that, as no formal battle has yet been arranged, with formal *défi*, between himself and Charles, Marsilie is still the legal holder (and challenger) of the fief; to accept the glove would be to publish abroad Marsilie's defeat and humiliation. Thus the poet finds courtesy even in the Emir of Cairo, who would spare Marsilie's feelings if he could.'

2849. Whitehead's edition contains the typographical error *tendut* for *rendut* ('lay aside').

2864. That is, on land as yet unconquered by him.

2924. *Califerne* is the only unidentified name on the list and is probably imaginary.

2973. We use 'precious' as having much the same force as the adjectival place name *galazin* whose meaning is unknown.

2997. Literally, 'one hundred thousand men looking on'. His whole army numbers 350,000.

3003. Literally, 'they are mounted and they have great skill'.

3093. The *oriflamme* (see note to vv. 3266–7) is a banner presumably representing what was Charlemagne's eventual historical rank as Holy Roman Emperor. In fact it was the name applied to the red banner of the abbey of Saint Denis which the French kings first carried in the eleventh century.

3135. Literally, 'now I hear great courage [spoken]'.

3146. We supply here a logical line for the assumed blank in the ms.

3157. Literally, 'he has a wide crutch (crotch)', a standard form of description.

3169. The words 'the pagans cry' are in the preceding line.

3179. It is possible to interpret this line as affirmative.

3182. We add 'here today' to clarify the meaning.

3197. These troops are called *enfanz*, young squires hoping to win knighthood on the field.

3212. Literally, 'in such an hour that'.

3226. The ms says *de Sorbres e de Sorz* which are really two versions of the same name; hence our translation.

3241. The ms repeats 'of Persians' (*de pers*) from the previous line. We adopt Whitehead's 'fiery' (*engrés*).

3257. We fill the lacuna in the middle of this line.

3266ff. Although the situation is often confused in the *Roland*, some account of the various army banners is in order. Each leader has a *gonfanon*, sometimes called an *enseigne*, or personal pennant. Charles also has his *oriflamme* (see note to v. 3093). Baligant has a *dragon* (which Jenkins says, in a note to the line, is a dragon figure mounted on a staff), and also banners of Mahomet and Tervagant. A statue of Apollo is carried before Baligant. The word *enseigne* also means 'battle-cry'; in Charlemagne's case it is *Monijoie* and the name is given to his *oriflamme* (v. 3095); Baligant's cry is *Précïuse*, the name of his sword. Finally, each knight (Christian and pagan alike, apparently) could or did have his own *gonfanon* attached to his lance; we frequently read that a knight buried his *gonfanon* or *enseigne* in an opponent's body.

3278. We employ 'declared' for the mysterious *uucget* of the ms.

3295. He actually calls them 'my infidel race' but the sense is clear.

3325. Literally, 'he has said and set forth a speech to them'.

3367. We use 'pagans' for the mysterious *gent* ('people')
iesnie (?).

3390. Many editors assume a missing line here. We
supply the line suggested by Jenkins in preference to leaving
a blank.

3404. That is, Charlemagne.

3494. A lacuna is generally assumed here. We follow
Whitehead.

3555. Literally, 'they become more quiet'.

3624. The line is obscure. We conjecture.

3694. This refers to the notion that each of the names of
God has a special virtue and power and the practice of
reciting them in turn like a sort of litany.

3758. 'Says Ganelon' is in the preceding line.

3775. See note to v. 326.

3786. The line is incomplete in the ms. We conjecture.

3812. Literally, 'At the price of death no more will be
seen this ———' the last word in the ms being mysterious.
Assuming that Roland is indicated, we translate on the
model of vv. 3802-3.

3814. Charlemagne views the council's decision as morally
reprehensible and as a personal affront.

3816. We translate freely, adding 'for a long time he sits'.

3828. Literally, 'one should protect your service well'.

3832. An incomplete line in the ms. We conjecture.

3848. The pledges are at once hostages to guarantee the
champion's appearance at the trial and responsible for his
well-being until that time. In this case they turn out to be
hostages for the justice of his cause as well.

3919-20. These lines repeat the same ending in the ms.
We conjecture.

3955. Literally, 'you are dead and destroyed'.

3983. The ms calls the ladies *cruiz* and *linees*. We conjecture freely in the face of the controversy aroused by

these two words. Whitehead and Jenkins give accounts in their notes.

4002. Among the possible suggested meanings for this line we find: 'Here ends the poem (or source, or tale) which Turoldus is composing (or copying, or reciting)', '. . . for Turoldus is getting weak (or old)'. Where scholarship has failed, we renounce the attempt to influence the reader and leave him to his own devices.

GLOSSARY OF PROPER NAMES

This glossary is not exhaustive; easily recognizable modern names and Old French names given modern equivalents in the translation are not included. Only the first occurrence of each name is given. Speculative historical bases of names are not given, but geographical equivalents are mentioned where useful. Many of the exotic-sounding Saracen names lend themselves to speculation on possible puns, but this dangerous etymological speculation is likewise avoided.

Abisme. A Saracen lord. 1470

Acelin. Count of Gascony, a baron of Charlemagne. 172

Aëlroth. King Marsilie's nephew. 1188

Aix. Modern Aix-la-Chapelle (Aachen); seat of the Emperor Charlemagne. 36

Alde. Oliver's sister; Roland's fiancée. 1720

Alexandrine. Materials shipped from the Middle East, often from Alexandria, were commonly given this adjective. 408

Alfrere. A Saracen possession of Marganice. 1915

Almace. Archbishop Turpin's sword. 2089

Almaris (of Belferne). A Saracen king. 812

Alphaien. A Saracen duke. 1554.

Amborre (of Oluferne). Baligant's standard bearer. 3297

Anseïs. One of the Twelve Peers. 105

Antelme (de Maience). A baron of Charlemagne. 3008

Apollo. One of the 'gods' of Islam. 8

Ardennes. The wooded plateau in NE. France. 728.

Argoille. An imaginary or unidentified pagan land. 3259

Astor. A French baron. 796

Austorie. A French duke. 1625

Babylon. Modern Cairo. 2614

Balaguer. A Catalonian fortress. 200

Baldewin. Son of Count Ganelon. 314

Baldise. An imaginary or unidentified pagan city. 3255

Balide. An imaginary or unidentified pagan town. 3230

Baligant. Emir of Babylon (modern Cairo) and liege lord of Marsilie. 2614

Barbamusche. Climorin's war horse. 1534

Basan. French baron; brother of Basilie. Murdered with Basilie while serving as ambassador to Marsilie. 208

Basbrun. Officer of Charles' court or army. 3952

Bascle. An imaginary or unidentified Saracen place. 3474

Basilie. See Basan.

Berenger. One of the Twelve Peers. 795

Besgun. Charlemagne's chief cook. 1818

Bevon (of Belne and Digun). A French baron. Belne = modern Beaune, Digun = modern Dijon. 1891

Bire. An imaginary or unidentified land. 3995

Blaive. Modern Blaye-sur-Gironde. 3689

Blancandrin (de Castel de Valfunde). Principal adviser of King Marsilie and his ambassador to King Charlemagne. 13

Blos. A pagan people. 3224

Bramimonde. Queen of Spain, wife of Marsilie. Christened Juliane by Charles after her conversion. 634

Bruise. An imaginary or unidentified pagan land. 3245

Bruns. A pagan people. 3225

Burel. A Saracen lord. 1388.

Butentrot. A pagan land. (Butrinto in Epirus, the legendary birthplace of Judas Iscariot?) 3220

Calabre. Modern Calabria. 371

Califerne. See note to v. 2924

Caliph. His name is not given; Marsilie's uncle. 453

Canabeus. Saracen King of Floredée; Baligant's brother. 3312

Capuel. A pagan king. 1614

Carcassone. The mediaeval fortress whose walls stand today. 385

Cazmarine. A Saracen town, possibly Camariñas in Galicia. 956

Charlemagne, Charles. King of France, Emperor of the Franks. 1

Cheriant. An imaginary or unidentified Saracen place. 3208

Chernuble (de Munigre). A Saracen lord. 975

Clarbone. An imaginary or unidentified pagan land. 3259

Clariën. Baligant's ambassador to Charlemagne. 2670

Clarifan. Baligant's ambassador to Charlemagne. 2670

Clarin (de Balaguer). A Saracen lord and emissary to Charles. 63

Clavers. A Saracen people. 3245

Climorin. A Saracen lord. 627

Col de Size. The pass through the Pyrenees between Pampeluna and Saint-Jean-Pied-de-Port. 2939

Commibles. A town in the Iberian Peninsula (= Coimbras?). 198

Cordres. Modern Córdoba. 71

Corsalis. A Saracen king. 885

Dapamort. A Saracen king from Lycia. 3205

Dathan and *Abirun.* Two rulers destroyed by God for rebellion (*Numbers* XVI, 1–35). 1215

Droün. Uncle of Gualter del Hum. 2048

Durendal. Roland's sword. 926

Durestant. An unidentified Spanish town marking the southern limits of the old Christian kingdoms of Spain. 870

Enfruns. A pagan people. 3518

Engeler (of Bordeaux). One of the Twelve Peers. 1289

Escababi. A Saracen lord. 1555

Escremiz (of Valterne). A Saracen lord. 931

Espaneliz. A Saracen lord in Baligant's army. 2648

Esperveres. A Saracen lord. 1388

Estamarin. A Saracen lord and emissary to Charlemagne. 64

Estramariz. A Saracen lord. 941

Esturgan. A Saracen lord. 940

Esturguz. A Saracen lord. 1358

Eudropin. A Saracen lord and emissary to Charlemagne. 64

Eugiez. A pagan people. 3243.

Faldrun (de Pui). A Saracen lord. 1871

Falsaron. Brother of King Marsilie. 879

Fleurit. A Saracen king. 3211

Franks. In the Oxford ms there is generally no distinction
between Franks (*li Franc*) and the French (*li Franceis*).
50

Fronde. An imaginary or unidentified pagan land. 3260

Gaifier. A French duke. 798

Gaignun. King Marsilie's war horse. 1890

Galafes. A Saracen emir. 1503

Galne. A Spanish town destroyed by Roland. 662

Ganelon. French count; stepfather of Roland; brother-in-
law of Charlemagne; ambassador to Marsilie. 178

Garmalie. A Saracen possession of Marganice. 1915

Gebuin. Commander of one of Charlemagne's first two
divisions against Baligant. 2432

Gemalfin. A Saracen knight, marshal of Baligant's army. 2814

Gerer. One of the Twelve Peers. 107

Gerin. One of the Twelve Peers. 107

Giles (Saint). The anchorite of Provence. 2096

Girart (de Rossillon). One of the Twelve Peers. 797

Godefroy (d'Anjou). Bearer of Charlemagne's gonfanon; brother of Tierri, Charlemagne's defender against Pinabel. 106

Godselme. Joint commander of Charlemagne's seventh division. 3067

Gramimund. The pagan Valdabrun's war horse. 1571

Grandonie. A pagan lord from Cappadocia; son of Capuel. 1613

Gros. A pagan people. 3229

Grossaille. A Saracen king. 1488.

Gualter (del Hum). Vassal of Roland; commander of the flank scouts at Rencesvals. 800

Guarlun. A Saracen lord. 65

Guineman. A French baron. 3014

Guinemer. Uncle of Count Ganelon. 348

Guitsand. Variant spelling of Wissant, an embarkation point for England between Boulogne and Calais. 1429

Guiun (de Saint-Antoine). A French baron. 1624

Halteclere. Oliver's sword. 1363

Haltilie. A Spanish town near which Basan and Basilie were murdered by Marsilie. 209

Hamon (de Galice). Joint commander of Charlemagne's eighth division. 3073

Henry. Nephew of Richard the Old of Normandy. 171

Herman (of Trace). French duke, commander of Charlemagne's fourth division. 3042

Imphe. An imaginary or unidentified town. 3996
Ives. One of the Twelve Peers. 1895
Ivoeries. One of the Twelve Peers. 1895

Jangleu. A chief counsellor to Baligant. 3507
Joiuse. Charlemagne's sword. 2501
Joüner. A Saracen lord and emissary to Charlemagne. 67
Jozeran (de Provence). Baron of Charlemagne; with Naimes, marshal of the army against Baligant. 3007
Jurfaleu (le Blond). Son and heir of King Marsilie. 504
Justin (de Valferrée). A Saracen baron. 1370

Lechs. Considered a pagan people. 3258
Lorain. Commander, with Gebuin, of one of the first two divisions against Baligant. 3022
Louis. Louis the Pious, son of Charlemagne. 3715

Machiner. Saracen lord, nephew of Maheu and emissary to Charlemagne. 66
Maëlgut. A Saracen baron. 2047
Maheu. Saracen lord, uncle of Machiner and emissary to Charlemagne. 66
Mahomet, Mahom. One of the 'gods' of Islam. 8
Malbien. Saracen lord and emissary to Charlemagne. 67
Malduit. Treasurer to King Marsilie. 642
Malpalin (of Narbonne). A Saracen killed by Charlemagne years before. 2995
Malpramis. Son of Baligant. 3176
Malpreis. An imaginary pagan land. 3253

Malprimis (de Brigant). A Saracen lord. 889

Malquiant. A Saracen lord, son of Malquid. 1594

Maltét. Baligant's lance. 3152

Maltraien. A Saracen king, father of Clarifan and Clarïen. 2671

Malun. A Saracen lord. 1353

Marbrise and *Marbrose.* Two imaginary ports at the mouth of the River Ebro. 2641

Marbrose. See 'Marbrise'. 2641

Marcule. A Saracen lord. 3156

Marganice. Uncle of King Marsilie. 1914

Margariz (de Sebilie). A Saracen lord. 'Margariz' is a common noun meaning 'a convert from Christianity'. 955

Marmorie. The war horse of the pagan Grandonie. 1615

Marsilie. Saracen King of Spain, vassal of the Emir Baligant. 7

Marsune. An imaginary or unidentified place. 2994

Maruse. An imaginary or unidentified pagan place. 3257

Micenes. The Milceni, a Slavonic people in Baligant's army. 3221

Michael (Saint). The Archangel Saint Michael. See also 'Mont Saint Michel'. 37

Milun. French noble, cousin of Tedbald de Reins. 173

Mont Saint Michel du Péril de la Mer. The monastery on the NW. coast of France. 1428

Moriane. The modern valley of Maurienne? 909

Murgleis. Ganelon's sword. 346

Naimes. French duke, principal adviser to Charlemagne. 230

Nerbone. Modern Arbonne, a town in the Basque country. 3683

Nevelon. Breton Count, shares command of Charlemagne's sixth division. 3057

Noples. A Spanish town (modern Napal?). 198

Nubles. A pagan people. 3224

Occian. An imaginary or unidentified pagan land. 3246

Oedun. Lord of the Bretons. 3056

Oger. Duke of Denmark, baron of Charlemagne. 170

Oliver. French Count; comrade of Roland; one of the Twelve Peers. 104

Oluferne. Modern Aleppo? 3297

Ormaleus. A pagan people. 3243

Otes, Otun. French Baron, one of the Twelve Peers. 795. Also another baron, 2432

Passecerf. Count Gerer's war horse. 1380

Petchenegs. A fierce Tartar people from the Black Sea. 3241

Pinabel (de Castel de Sorence). A member of Ganelon's family and the latter's champion at his trial. 362

Pine. District conquered by Roland. Area about San Juan de la Peña near Jaca? 199

Précïuse. Baligant's sword. 3146

Priamum. Saracen lord and emissary to Charlemagne. 65

Primes. An imaginary or unidentified Saracen place. 967

Puille. Modern Apulia. 371

Rabel. A French Baron. 3014

Reiner. French Duke, father of Oliver. 2208

Rembalt. Joint commander of Charlemagne's eighth division. 3073

Rencesvals. Modern Roncevaux, at a junction on the main road from Pampeluna to Saint-Jean-Pied-de-Port. Site of the historical ambush of the rearguard on 15th August 778, during the return of Charlemagne's Spanish expedition. 892

Richard the Old. Norman noble; commander of Charlemagne's sixth division. 171

Roland. French count; nephew of Charlemagne; step-son of Ganelon; one of the Twelve Peers. Based on Rolandus, Count of the Breton March, slain at Roncevaux.

Saltperdut. The war horse of the Saracen Malquiant. 1597

Samuel (Tsar). Possibly refers to a Bulgarian tsar of the tenth century. 3244

Sansun. French duke, one of the Twelve Peers. 105

Saracen. A general term meaning Arab or Moslem. 147

Saragoce. Modern Saragossa. The capital of the Saracen king Marsilie. 6

Sebilie. Modern Seville? 955

Seinz. Variously identified as Xanten in Westphalia or Saintes. 1428

Sezilie. Modern Seville? 200

Siglorel. A Saracen sorcerer. 1390

Sizer. See 'Col de Size'. 583

Soltras. A pagan people. 3242

Sorbres. A pagan Slavonic people. 3226

Sorel. Count Gerin's war horse. 1379

Strymonis. A pagan people. 3258

Suatilie. An imaginary or unidentified pagan country. 90

Tachebrun. Ganelon's war horse. 347

Tedbald de Reins. A baron of Charlemagne. 173

Tencendur. Charlemagne's war horse. 2993

Tervagant. One of the three 'gods' of Islam. 611

Tierri. Brother of Godefroy d'Anjou; champion of Charlemagne at Ganelon's trial. 2884

Tierri (of Argonne). Commander of Charlemagne's ninth division. 3083

Timozel. A Saracen lord. 1382

Torleu. A pagan king from Persia. 3204

Tüele. Modern Tudela, above Saragossa on the River Ebro. 200

Turgis (de Turteluse). A Saracen baron. 916

Turoldus. The author or scribe of the poem, of some source or of the Oxford ms. 4002

Turpin (de Reins). Archbishop of Rheims. 170

Val Ferrée. An imaginary Saracen place. 1370. Other names on the same model are: Val Füit 3239, Val Marchis 3208, Val Metas 1502, Val Penuse 3256, Val Sevrée 3313, Val Tenebrus 2461

Valdabrun. A Saracen lord. 617

Valterne. A Spanish town (modern Valterra?). 199

Veillantif. Roland's war horse. 1153

Vienne. Variously identified as Vienne on the Rhone or Viana in Galicia. 997

Vivien. A Christian king to be rescued by Charlemagne. 3996

Willalme (de Blaive). A baron of Charlemagne. 3938